A Color Guide to the 2022 iPad and iPad Pro For Seniors

A GUIDE TO THE IPAD (WITH IPADOS 16) WITH COLOR GRAPHICS

Scott La Counte

RIDICULOUSLY SIMPLE BOOKS

ANAHEIM, CALIFORNIA

www.RidiculouslySimpleBooks.com

Table of Contents

Disclaimer: Please note, while every effort has been made to ensure accuracy, this book is not endorsed by Apple, Inc. and should be considered unofficial.

INTRODUCTION

The iPad is more powerful than many laptops. But it's not a laptop. Using it can be a learning curve when you've never had a tablet.

The goal of this book is to help you uncover the iPad's most powerful features, so you can start using it as quickly as possible.

The **full color** guide is great for new iPad users and users who are upgrading from older models.

Seeing images in B&W is helpful, but over the years, I've discovered that many readers prefer to see them in full color as they appear in real life; this manual was created from a B&W version that I am also selling.

Inside you'll learn about:

- Multitasking
- Widgets
- Quick Note
- FaceTime
- Messages
- Focus
- Notifications
- Stage Manager
- Safari
- Maps
- Photos

- And More

Are you ready to start enjoying your new iPad? Then let's get started

Chapter 1: Let's Get Started

iPad vs. iPad

There's really four iPads when it comes to Apple: the iPad Pro, iPad Air, iPad Mini, and iPad. Only the iPad Pro and iPad were refreshed in 2022. As the name implies, the iPad Pro is their highest end tablet and suited for people who don't use it casually—animators, business professionals, etc. The regular iPad can do some serious work, but it's targeted to the casual user—the person who uses it to watch movies, check Facebook, and maybe play the occasional game.

The 2022 iPad is slightly larger in screen size (10.9 inch vs. 10.2 inch); it's also using a faster processor (A14 vs A13). While the front cameras haven't been upgraded, the back ones have (12MP vs. 8MP). The new iPad is just a smidgen lighter than the previous model (1.05 pounds vs. 1.07). Apple has also decided to ditch the lightning cable on the iPad and switched to USB-C.

When it comes to comparing the iPad Pro 2022 vs. the 2021, the differences are a lot smaller; the biggest difference is the iPad Pro 2022 has a M2 chip (the previous model has a M1); what does that mean? It's fast. Really fast! More than 35% faster than last year's model. If you just use your iPad to check email, that's not going to mean a lot; but if you are using it to do video editing, you'll love the difference. The iPad Pro is made for the power user, and if that's you, you'll be happy with the latest M2 chip.

The Apple Keyboard and Apple Pencil

You may have bought the iPad but haven't made your mind up about the Keyboard and Pencil. So, let's talk about both of those things briefly.

The Keyboard is, well, a keyboard! But if you've had the old Apple Keyboard case, then one thing you'll probably be happy about is that old origami style is gone; maybe it's just me, but I always had a hard time figuring out how to fold it! This one is much simpler.

Simpler means one position is gone; on the previous version, it could be used as a stand without the Keyboard. Not the case anymore. It, of course, stands up with the Keyboard open.

It also has two positions, so you can have two viewing angles; this is helpful when you are typing on your lap, but not as functional as the keyboard case with more limitless possibilities with the position.

It's not terribly heavy, but it does add some weight; I recommend testing it at a store before buying.

Next, the Apple Pencil; I'll cover this more later in the book, but I do want to point out that the Pencil is pretty basic for this generation. It's completely redesigned, and it no longer comes with "tips." You have to buy those extra. They're pretty cheap though.

The biggest advantage of the new Apple Pencil is you don't have to plug it in. The previous generation had to be charged at the bottom of the iPad in the charging port, which really could get in the way. This generation is all magnetic.

The 2022 iPad is only compatible with the first generation Pencil (which does not magnetically charge); the iPad Pro is compatible with the first and second generation pencil.

Let's Talk About Your Face

Let's talk briefly about your face. Don't worry—your gorgeous! What I'm talking about is Face ID. You may be used to using that on your phone—it's a great feature. You may have even heard about the feature on some of the iPad's. So where is it? Unless you got a new iPad, you won't find it. Fingerprint sensor is all you get. So if you are looking around the iPad trying to find it, then let me save you the trouble: Face ID isn't there.

What's New In iPadOS 16?

iPadOS is an interesting thing: it's a little bit iOS and a little bit macOS--that means if you have a Macbook and iPhone, and have upgraded to the latest OS, many of these features you've probably already used. If you are invested into Apple's ecosystem, then you'll love how familiar all their devices are—yes, they're different sizes and shapes, but the features on one are often nearly identical on others. If you use a Mac, you'll probably find that iPadOS is becoming more and more like a Mac experience.

Sharing photos is easier than ever; a new feature lets you share photos with family and friends automatically; you can even set up rules with start dates and people to determine what is shared and when. So, for example, if you are going to a wedding on a certain date, you can set up the iPad to automatically start sharing on that date with others attending.

If you liked Tab Groups on iPadOS 15, you'll love it on 16; you can now share those tab groups with friends; so if, for example, you are planning a vacation with others, you can share a tab group so you are all on the same page.

Messages has several new features including editing a message (but only for the first 15 minutes); unsending a message (but only for the first two minutes), marking a message as unread, and recovering deleted messages up to 30 days later. With SharePlay for messages, you can also synchronize movies, music and more with friends over iMessage. Unsend messages also comes to the iPad mail app: Mail--in addition to schedule send, follow-up, and remind me.

One of the big highlights of iPadOS is Stage Manager. Stage Manager lets you resize apps into windows and makes it easier to multitask.

These are just some of the bigger upgrades, but there's smaller tweaks that will be covered in this book

Thanks for the Nice Gesture, Apple!

And now the moment you've been reading for: how to make your way around an iPad mini without the Home button.

Remember, these gestures are pretty universal—they work on the iPad mini and they work on iPhones that don't have the Home button.

Let's Go Home

First, the easiest gesture: getting to your Home screen. Do you have your pen and paper ready? It's complicated...swipe up from the bottom of your screen.

That's it.

It's not too far off from pushing a button. Heck, your finger's even in the same place! The only difference is you're moving your thumb upward instead of inward.

Multitask

As Dorothy would say, there's no place like Home—but we can still give a shout out to multitask, can't we? If you don't know what it is, multitask is how you switch quickly between apps—you're in iMessage and want to open up Safari to get a website, for example; instead of closing iMessage, finding Safari from the Home screen, and then repeating the process to get back, you use multitask to do it quickly.

On the old iPad's you would double press the Home button. On the new iPad mini, you Swipe Up from the bottom as if you were going to Home...but don't lift your finger; instead of lifting your finger, continue swiping up until you reach the middle of your screen—at this point, you should see the multitask interface.

If you have an app open (Note: this does not work on the Home screen), you can also slide your finger right across the bottom edge of the screen; this will go to the previous app open.

Mission Control...We're Go for Flashlight

If you haven't noticed, I'm putting these features in order of use. So, the third most common gesture people use is the Control Center. That's where all your Controls are located—go figure...Control is where controls are!

We'll go over the Control Center in more detail later in the book. For now, just know that this is where you'll do things like adjust brightness, enable airplane mode, and turn on the beloved flashlight. On the old iPad, you accessed Control Center by swiping up from the bottom of the screen. No Bueno on the new iPad mini—if you recall, swiping up gets you Home.

The new gesture for Control Center is swiping down from the upper right corner of the iPad mini (not the top middle, which will do something else).

Notify Me How to Get Notifications

Eck! So many gestures to remember! Let me throw you a bone. To see notifications (those are the alerts like email and text that you get on your tablet and phone), swipe down from the middle of the screen. That's the same way you did it before! Finally, nothing new to remember!

I hate to steal your bone back, but about not remembering anything new: there is something to remember. :-(

If you swipe down from the right corner, you get the Control Center; that wasn't the case on old iPads. Swiping down anywhere on top got you to the Home screen. On the new iPad mini, you can only swipe in the middle.

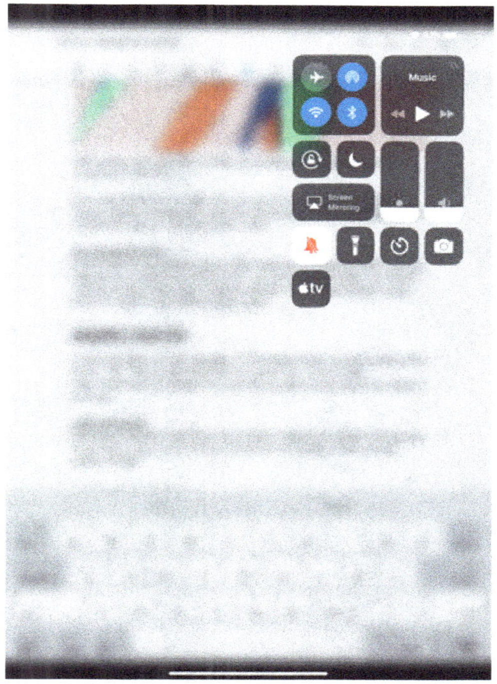

Searching for Answers

If you're like me, you probably have a million apps—and because you want to see the wallpaper on your iPad mini's Home screen, you put those million apps in one folder! That may not be the best way to organize a library, but the search function on the iPad mini, makes it easy to find anything quickly.

In addition to apps, you can use search to find calendar dates, contacts, things on the Internet—you can even search for text that appears in a photo.

The best part of search? Works the same way it does on older iPads...there's your bone back! From your Home screen, swipe down in the middle of the screen.

Calling All Widgets

So Widgets are one of the latest greatest things on the iPad. Amazing! What are they?! Think of it like mini software. It runs on your Home screen so you can see information without actually opening the app. If you have stocks, for example, it shows the value of stocks you pick in real time, so you don't have to open anything. The goal is just to save you a few seconds in the day—or, in the case of the Photo widget which shows memories of places you've gone or people you've met, brighten your day.

If you have an iPhone, you might already know how Widgets work because the concept is the same. First, tap and hold your finger over the Home screen; that's going to make icons jiggle and also put a + button up in the left corner. Next, tap that + button.

This brings up the Widgets that are available. As more developers make Widgets for their apps, you'll see this area grow. Remember, you only see Widgets for apps you have downloaded on your device; so, for example, if you don't have the Weather app, then you won't see the Weather widget.

Weather is a popular widget, so let's start by adding that one. Go to the Weather name on the left menu.

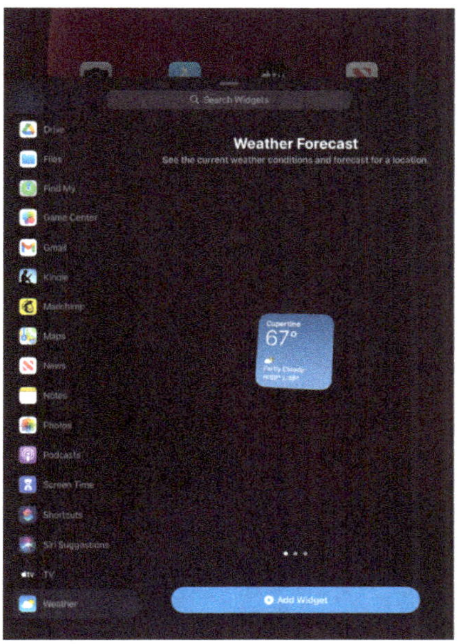

Under the preview, you'll see three dots; that indicates you can swipe to the right to see more. You'll notice the preview gets larger because the widget gets larger. The bigger the preview, the more space it will take on your Home screen. When you see the one you like, tap "Add Widget."

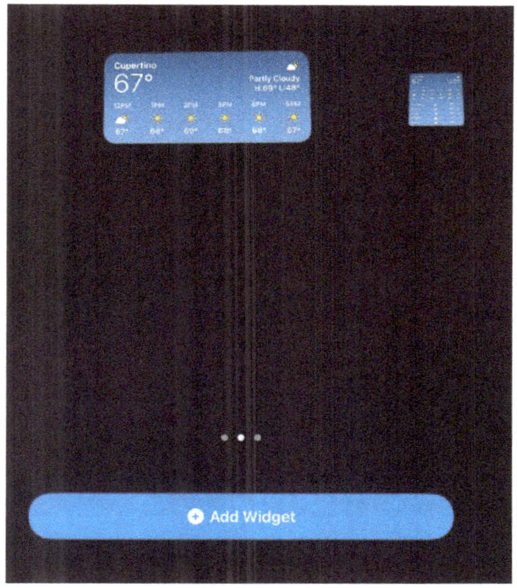

Some Widgets have things available on them to edit. If you tap and hold on the widget, you can see if there's more you can do. In the case of the Weather widget, you can change the location. Just tap on Cupertino (or whatever location currently shows on your device).

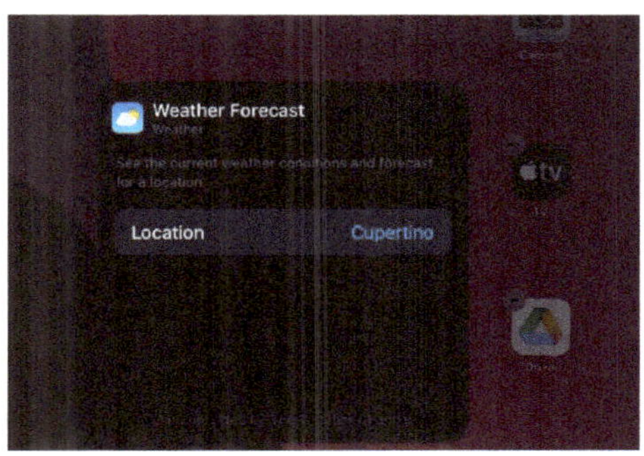

Next, either tap "My Location" to show the location your device currently is in (if you travel to a different location, it will automatically change), or select search and manually find the city you want to show.

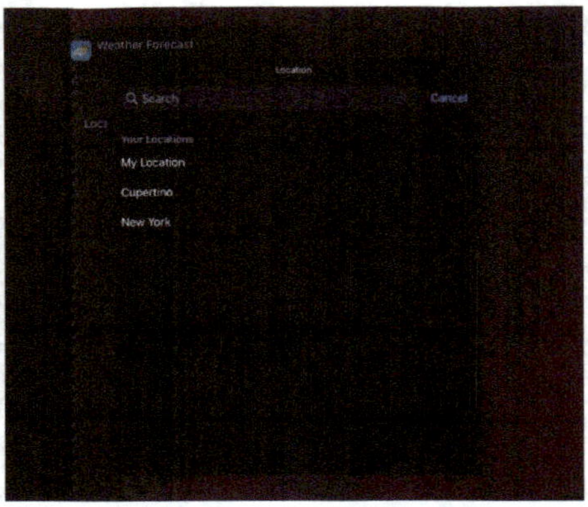

Once you select Done, your Widget will appear on the Home screen.

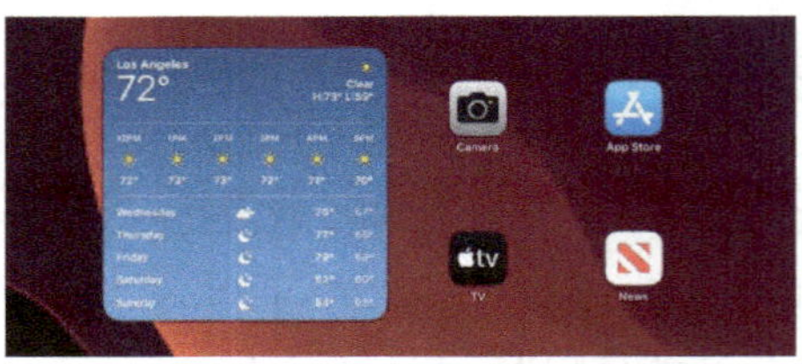

Smart Stacks

You can also add what's known as a Smart Stack as a widget. This is a widget that changes based on what it predicts you will use during one point in the day.

If the widget is the same size, you can drag it into another widget box to create your own Smart Stack.

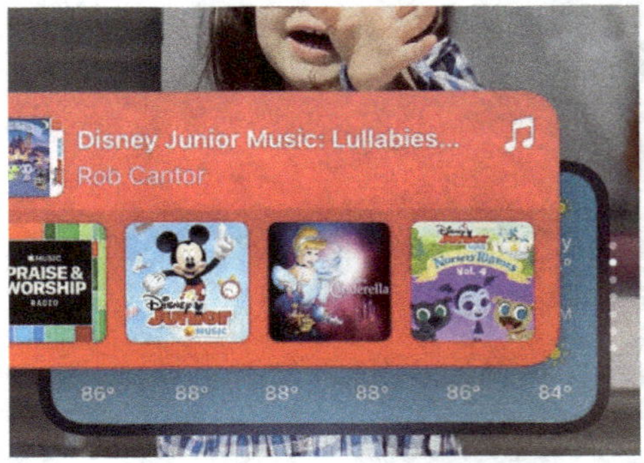

Once added, you can swipe up and down within that widget to toggle between the app.

If you long-press on it, you are able to edit the stack.

When you edit it, you can move what's in the stack and turn off Smart Rotate, so it doesn't rotate throughout the day.

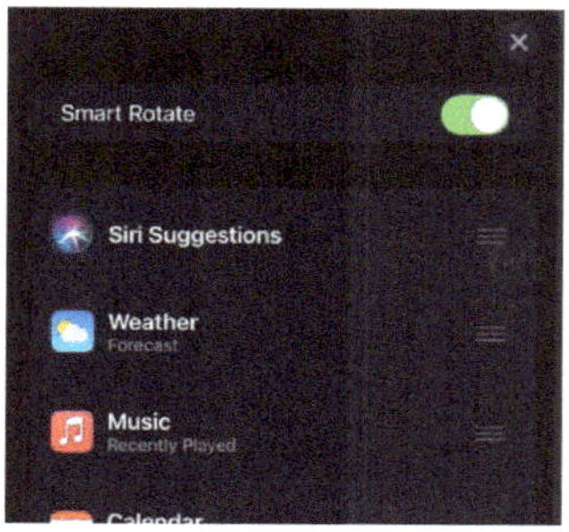
Smart Rotate
Siri Suggestions
Weather
Forecast
Music
Recently Played

Chapter 2: The Setup

Setting Up

I don't want to take away from the main topics to spend several pages setting up your iPad mini. The setup is straightforward, and the onscreen help gives you everything you need to know. There are a few things, however, you should know about the setup:

You can change things. If you say yes (or no) to something but change your mind, you'll be able to change it in the Settings, which I will walk you through in corresponding sections throughout this book.

If you are moving from an older iPad to the iPad mini and want to keep all of the settings, make sure to back it up before restoring it over the Cloud. To do this, go into Settings. Next, click your account name (first thing you'll see on top). Then iCloud and iCloud Backup (near the middle when you scroll), and finally Back Up Now.

Face ID - Face ID is probably new to you unless you have last year's iPhone X. One thing that's worth pointing out is you can add multiple faces. For example, if your spouse or child uses your tablet, they can add their face to Face ID and won't have to put in a passcode or ask you to unlock it every time they want to use it.

Gestures

Throughout the book, I'll refer to certain gestures. To make sure you understand the terminology, below are the most common ones:

Tap

This is the "click" of the iPad world. A tap is just a brief touch. It doesn't have to be hard or last very long. You'll tap icons, hyperlinks, form choices, and more. You'll also tap numbers on a touch keypad in order to make calls. It's not exactly rocket science, is it!

Tap and Hold

This simply means touching the screen and leaving your finger in contact with the glass. It's useful for bringing up context menus or other options in some apps.

Double Tap

This refers to two rapid taps, like double clicking with your finger. Double tapping will perform different functions in different apps. It will also zoom in on pictures or webpages.

Swipe

Swiping means putting your finger on the surface of your screen and dragging it to a certain point and then removing your finger from the surface. You'll use this motion to navigate through menu levels in your apps, through pages in Safari, and more. It'll become second nature overnight, I promise.

Drag

This is mechanically the same as swiping, but with a different purpose. You'll touch an object to select it, and then drag it to wherever it needs to go and release it. It's just like dragging and dropping with a mouse, but it skips the middleman.

Pinch

Take two fingers, place them on the iPad mini screen, and move them either toward each other or away from each other in a pinching or reverse pinching motion. Moving your fingers together will zoom in inside many apps, including web browsers and photo viewers; moving them apart will zoom out.

Rotate and Tilt

Many apps on iPad mini take advantage of rotating and tilting the device itself. For instance, in the paid app Star Walk, you can tilt the screen so that it's pointed at whatever section of the night sky you're interested in—Star Walk will reveal the constellations based on the direction the iPad mini is pointed.

Emojis

The reason you shelled out $100s for an iPad mini that's more powerful than many computers was to send out adorable emojis in your text messages, right? Okay...maybe not! But the keyboard, and by extension emojis, is something you use a lot with your iPad, so it's worth learning more about it before digging deeper into the software that relies on them.

Anytime you type a message, the keyboard pops up automatically. There are no extra steps. But there are some things you can do with the keyboard to make it more personal.

There are a few things to notice on the keyboard—the delete key is marked with a little 'x' (it's right next to the letter M), and the shift key is the key with the upward arrow (next to the letter Z).

By default, the first letter you type will be capitalized. You can tell what case the letters are in though at a quick glance.

To use the shift key, just tap it and then tap the letter you want to capitalize or the alternate punctuation you'd like to use. Alternatively, you can touch the shift key and drag your finger to the letter you want to capitalize. Double tap the shift key to enter caps lock (i.e. everything is capitalized) and tap once to exit caps lock.

Special Characters

To type special characters, just tap and hold the key of the associated letter until options pop up. Drag your finger to the character you want to use and be on your way. What exactly would you use this for? Let's say you're are writing something in Spanish and need the accent on the "e"; tapping and holding on the "e" will bring that option up.

Using Dictation

Let's face it: typing on the keyboard stinks sometimes! Wouldn't be easier to just say what you want to write? If that sounds like you, then Dictation can help! Just tap the microphone next to the spacebar and start talking. It works pretty well.

Number and Symbol Keyboards

Of course, there's more to life than letters and exclamation points. If you need to use numbers, tap the 123 key in the bottom left corner. This will bring up a different keyboard with numbers and punctuation.

From this keyboard, you can get back to the alphabet by tapping the ABC key in the bottom left corner. You can also access an additional keyboard which includes the remaining standard symbols by tapping the #+- key, just above the ABC key.

Emoji Keyboard

And finally, the moment you've waited for! Emojis!

The emoji keyboard is accessible using the smiley face key between the 123 key and the dictation key. Emojis are tiny cartoon images that you can use to liven up your text messages or other written output. This goes far beyond the colon-based emoticons of yesteryear—there are enough emojis on your iPad mini to create an entire visual vocabulary.

To use the emoji keyboard, note that there are categories along the bottom (and that the globe icon on the far left will return you to the world of language). Within those categories, there are several screens of pictographs to choose from. Many of the human emojis include multicultural variations. Just press and hold them to reveal other options.

Multilingual Typing

Most people are probably all set. They know all they need to know about typing on the iPad and they're ready to blast emojis at their friends. There are a few other features that apply to some (not all people)

One such feature is Multilingual Typing. This is for people who type multiple languages at the same time. So, if you type between Spanish and English, you won't keep seeing a message saying your spelling is wrong.

If that sounds like you, then you just need to enable another dictionary, which is simple. Go to Settings > General > Dictionary.

Configuring International Keyboards

If you find yourself typing in a different language fairly often, you may want to set up international keyboards. To set up international keyboards, visit Settings > General > Keyboard > Keyboards. You can then add an appropriate international keyboard by tapping Add New Keyboard. As an example, iPad mini has great support for Chinese text entry—choose from pinyin, stroke, zhuyin, and handwriting, where you actually sketch out the character yourself.

When you enable another keyboard, the smiley emoji key will change to a globe icon. To use international keyboards, tap the globe key to cycle through your keyboard choices.

Your iPad mini is loaded with features to help prevent slip-ups, including Apple's battle-tested autocorrect feature, which guards against common typos. In iOS 8, Apple introduced a predictive text feature that predicts what words you're most likely to type, and its accuracy is even better in the new iPadOS.

Three choices appear just above the keyboard—the entry as typed, plus two best guesses. Predictive text is somewhat context-specific, too. It learns your speech patterns as you email your boss or text your best friend, and it will serve up appropriate suggestions based on who you're messaging or emailing. Of course, if it bothers you, you can turn it off by visiting Settings > General > Keyboards and turning off predictive text by sliding the green slider to the left.

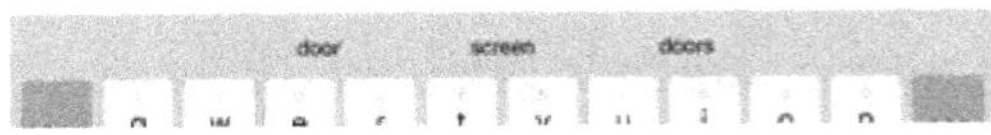

Chapter 3: The iPad Crash Course

Welcome Home

There's one thing that has pretty much stayed the same since the very first iPad was released: The Home screen. The look has evolved (and the dock on the bottom has changed a little), but the layout has not. All you need to know about it is it's the main screen. So, when you read me say "go to the Home screen" this is the screen I'm talking about. Make sense?

The Dock

The dock is the bottom portion of your Home screen.

This is where you can "dock" the apps you love and use the most. If you've used an older iPad or iPhone, then I'm sure you know all about it. But this dock is a little different.

Look at the above screenshot. Now look to the right. See that line? If not, look at the one below:

The apps to the right of that line are not put there by you. These are the last three apps you've used. So, these will always be changing. It helps you multitask much quicker.

App Library

If you've used your iPad or iPhone long enough, you probably have had an organization problem at some point. It's easy to fall in love with apps and before long you have dozens—if not hundreds—of them!

That's all well and good…until you have to find them! iPad fixes this with App Library. App Library lets you hide icons for apps you don't use as often. So they're still installed, but they don't clutter your screens.

You find the App Library by swiping left until you reach the last screen. The icons are all grouped together to help you find them easier, but you can also search for them in the search bar. Also, remember this is all your apps—even the ones you didn't hide.

There's also an App Library icon in your Dock. Tap that and it expands to all your apps.

This is all great, but how do you actually hide the apps? It's not too unlike deleting apps. First, tap and hold your screen until a minus icon appears on your icons (hint:

this only applies to icons NOT in your Dock—the ones in your Dock will only be removed from your Dock if you tap it).

When you tap the app, you will be asked if you want to "Delete App" or "Remove from Home Screen." You want "Remove from Home Screen," as deleting the app removes it from your device entirely. Once you do that, it's gone! It now resides in the App Library. To get it back, go to the App Library and drag it back out.

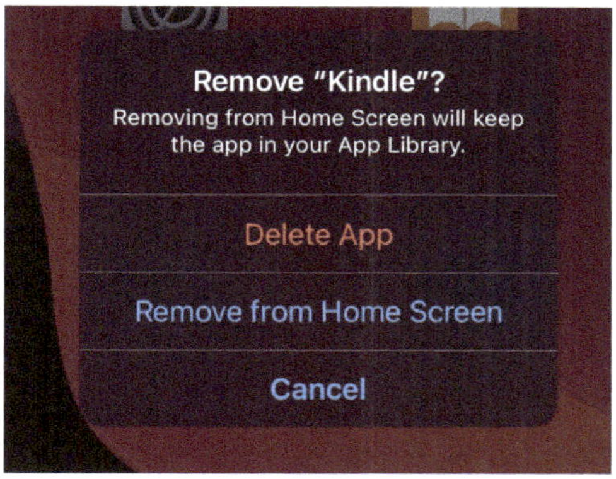

If you want to quick hide an entire screen, tap and hold your screen, then tap the two dots near the bottom.

You can uncheck any screen you want to hide—but you do need to keep one screen unhidden.

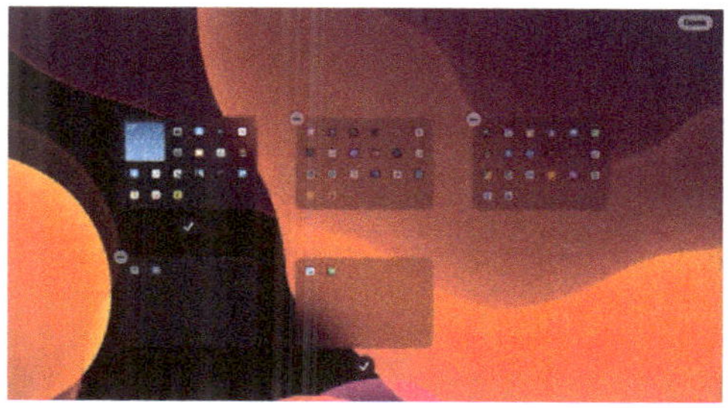

You can also remove the entire page, which will put all the apps in the App Library.

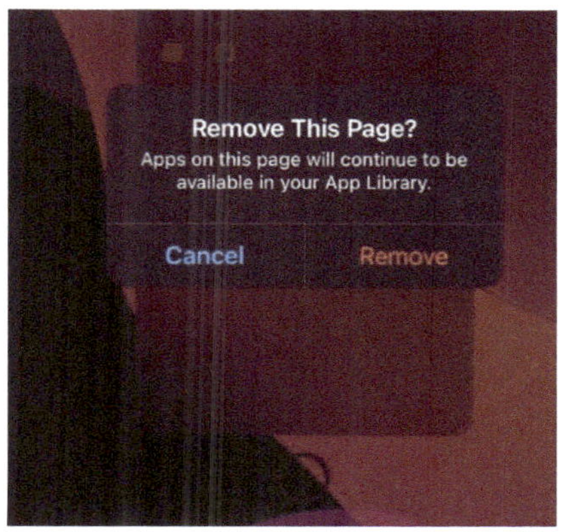

Making Calls

Your iPad mini is a great phone.

You read that right! In addition to thousands of other things, your iPad mini can make phone calls. It does this two ways:

1. **Over Wi-Fi with FaceTime Audio**
2. **With your iPhone**

There are a number of ways you can make calls:

If you are on a website or map and there's a phone number with a hyperlink, that means you can tap it and it will dial the number. Note: to do this, you have to have an iPhone tethered to your iPad mini. The call will come from your iPhone's phone number.

If someone sends you an iMessage on your iPad (we'll cover iMessage later in this chapter), you can tap that name and tap FaceTime Audio; the call will be made using FaceTime Audio.

The Contacts app has a list of all your contacts (hence the app's name!); any contact who has an iPhone that's tied to the given email will have a FaceTime Audio option—or, if your iPhone is tethered to your iPad mini, an option to dial them directly.

Receiving a call is fairly intuitive. If your iPad mini is tied to your iPhone, and the phone is in range of the iPad mini, then the call will come to your iPad mini as well. Swipe to answer. That's it.

FaceTime

How do you keep people together when they are apart? This is something Apple has thought deeply about. FaceTime on the iPad looks better than ever. Later in fall 2021, you will be able to watch movies together, listen to music together, and even troubleshoot device problems by sharing your iPad screen. It's called SharePlay. Unfortunately, some of these features are coming later in the fall, so this instructional guide cannot include them at this writing.

To get started open the FaceTime app; you have two options: Create Link or New FaceTime Call.

The Create Link button will give you a sharable link that you can give out to people. What's really cool about this is it can be shared with people who don't have iPhones—so they can open it inside Chrome on a Windows computer.

If you prefer to call someone directly, then tap the green New FaceTime button and type in their name.

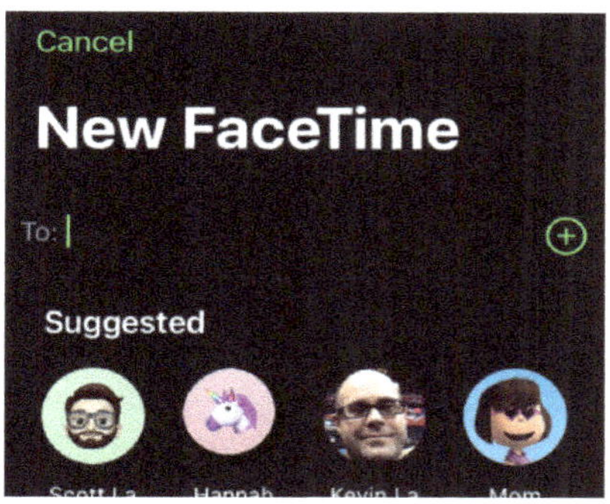

Your preview box is in the lower corner, but it can be moved anywhere on the screen by tapping and holding it, then dragging.

If you make this preview box larger, there's several options you have. In the upper left corner, you have a little image icon—that makes your background blurred or not blurred. The lower right will flip your camera from the front facing camera to back. The lower middle icon turns on and off Center Stage—Center Stage is a feature found on newer iPads; it follows you as you move, so if you move a little bit, the camera pans to follow you. The lower left corner will bring up effects you can add in.

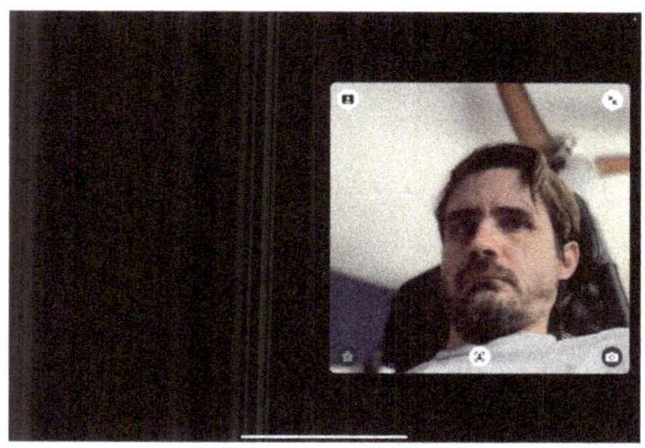

Effects can be moved around by tapping and holding or enlarged by pinching on them.

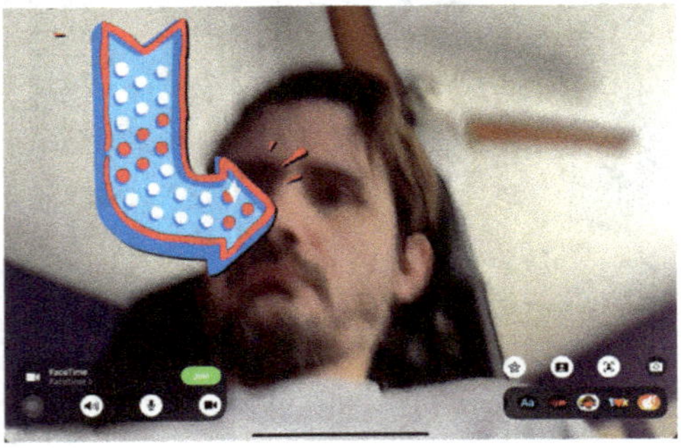

When you tap the screen, you'll also have a floating box with more controls. If you haven't started the call yet, for example if someone calls you on FaceTime, then you have to accept it, then tap the Join button; if you are on the call, then this button turns to a leave button—tap that to hang up. From left to right, the other buttons are Messages to send everyone on the call a message, Speaker if you want to transfer the sound to something like a HomePod, Microphone if you want to turn off your mic so they can't hear you, and Camera, which is where you go to turn off your video—they can hear you but not see you.

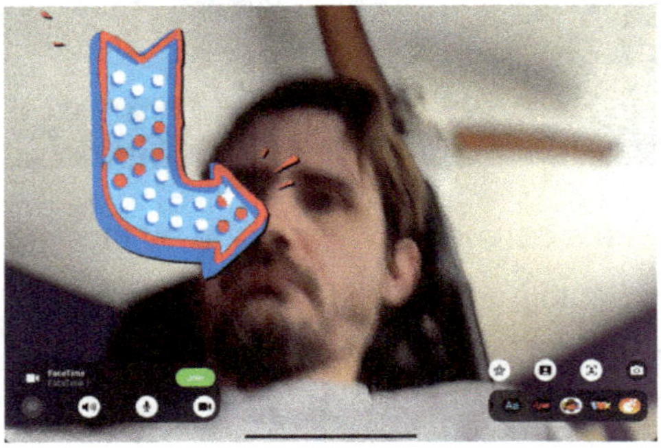

There's An App for That

App is short for application. So, when you hear the term "There's an app for that," it just means there's a program that does what you want to do. If you're a Windows user, all those things you always open (like Word and Excel) are apps. Apple has literally millions of apps. Opening an app is as simple as touching it.

Unlike apps on a computer, you don't have to close apps on your iPad. It's all automatic. For most apps, it will even remember where you were so when you open it again, it's saved.

Organizing Apps

If you're like me—and pretty much most people are—you love your apps and you have a lot of them! So, you'll need to know how to move them around, put them in folders, and delete them. It's all easy to do.

The Home screen may be the first screen you see, but if you swipe to the right, you'll see there are more. Personally, I keep the most used apps on the first screen, and not-so-used apps in folders on the second. The bottom dock is where I put the apps I use all the time (like Mail and Safari).

To rearrange apps, take your finger and touch one of your apps and hold it there until the icon jiggles. When the apps are jiggling like that, you can touch them without opening them and drag them around your screen. Try it out! Just touch an app and drag your finger to move it. When you've found the perfect spot, lift your finger and the app drops into place. After you've downloaded more apps, you can also drag apps across Home screens.

You can delete an app using the same method for moving them. The only difference is instead of moving them, you tap the 'x' in the upper left corner of the icon. Don't worry about deleting something on accident. Apps are stored in the Cloud. You can delete and install them as many times as you want; you don't have to pay again—you just have to download them again.

Putting apps on different screens is helpful, but to be really organized you want to use folders. You can, for example, have a folder for all your game apps, finance apps, social apps, whatever you want. You pick what to name it. If you want an "Apps I use on the toilet" folder, then you can absolutely have it!

To create a folder, just drag one app over another app you'd like to add into that folder.

Once they are together, you can name the folder. To delete the folder, just put the folder apps in "jiggle mode" and drag them out of the folder. iPad mini doesn't allow empty folders—when a folder is empty, iPad mini deletes it automatically.

Messaging

More and more tablet users are staying connected through text messages instead of phone calls, and the iPad mini makes it easy to keep in touch with everyone. You can also use iMessage to interact with other Apple users. This feature allows you to send instant messages to anyone signed into a Mac running OS X Mountain Lion or higher, or any iOS device running iOS 5 or greater. iMessage for iPadOS has been completely changed to make everything just a little more...animated.

On the main Messages screen, you will be able to see the many different conversations you have going on. You can also delete conversations by swiping from right to left on the conversation you'd like and tapping the red Delete button. New conversations or existing conversations with new messages will be highlighted with a big blue dot next to it, and the Messages icon will have a badge displaying the number of unread messages you have, similar to the Mail and iPhone icons.

To create a message, click on the Messages icon, then the Compose button in the top right corner.

Once the new message dialog box pops up, click on the plus button (+) to choose from your contacts list, or just type in the phone number of the person you wish to text. For group messages, just keep adding as many people as you'd like. Finally, click on the bottom field to begin typing your message.

iMessage has added in a lot of new features over the past few years. If all you want to do is send a message, then just tap the blue up arrow.

But you can do so much more than just send a message! (Please note, if you are sending a message with newer features to someone with an older OS or a non-Apple device, then it won't look as it appears on your screen).

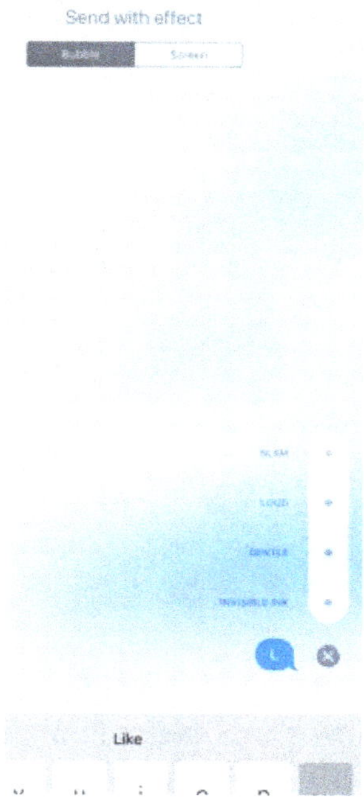

On the top of this screen, you'll also notice two tabs; one says "Bubble" and the other says "Screen"; if you tap Screen you can add animations to the entire screen. Swipe right and left to see each new animation.

When you get a message that you like, and you want to respond to it, you can tap and hold your finger over the message or image; this will bring up different ways you can react.

Once you make your choice, the person on the receiving end will see how you responded.

If you'd like to add animation, a photo, a video, or lots of other things, then let's look at the options next to the message.

You have three choices—which bring up even more choices! The first is the camera, which lets you send photos with your message (or take new photos—note, these photos won't be saved on your iPad mini), the next lets you use iMessage apps (more on that in a second), and the last lets you record a message with your voice.

Let's look at the camera option first.

If you want to take an original photo, then tap the round button on the bottom. To add effects, tap the star in the lower left corner.

Tapping effects brings up all the different effects available to you. I'll talk more about Animoji soon but as an example, this app lets you put an Animoji over your face (see the example below—not bad for an author photo, eh?!)

Finally, the last option is apps. You should know all about iPad mini apps by now, but now there's a new set of apps called iMessage apps. These apps let you be both silly (send digital stickers) and serious (send cash to someone via text). To get started, tap the '+' button to open the iMessage App Store.

You can browse all the apps just like you would the regular App Store. Installing them is the same as well.

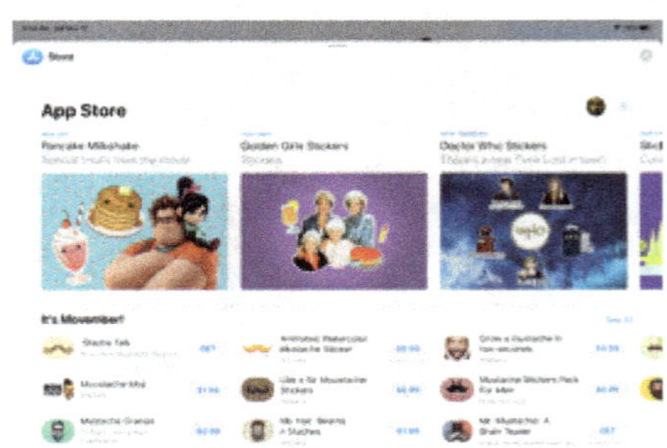

When you're ready to use the app, just tap apps, tap the app you want to load, and tap what you want to send. You can also drag stickers on top of messages. Just tap, hold and drag.

Also, in the app section is a button called #images.

If you tap on this button you can search for thousands of humorous memes and animated GIFs. Just tap it and search a term you want to find—such as "Money" or "Fight".

One final iMessage feature worth trying out is the personal handwritten note. Tap on a new message like you are going to start typing a new message; now rotate your tablet horizontally. This brings up an option to use your finger to create a handwritten note. Sign away, and then hit done when you're finished.

Message Tagging

If you have used messaging programs like Slack, then you are probably all too familiar with tagging someone in a conversation. Tagging gets the person's attention and starts a new thread within the conversation.

So if you are in a large text message exchange, then when you tag someone, everyone can read it, but everyone is not notified. So it's a little less unobtrusive.

To tag someone in a conversation, just put an @ in front of their name when you reply.

If you want to reply in-line to a message, then long-press the message. By in-line, I mean this: let's say there's a message several texts up—you can long-press to reply to it, so they know what message you are referring to.

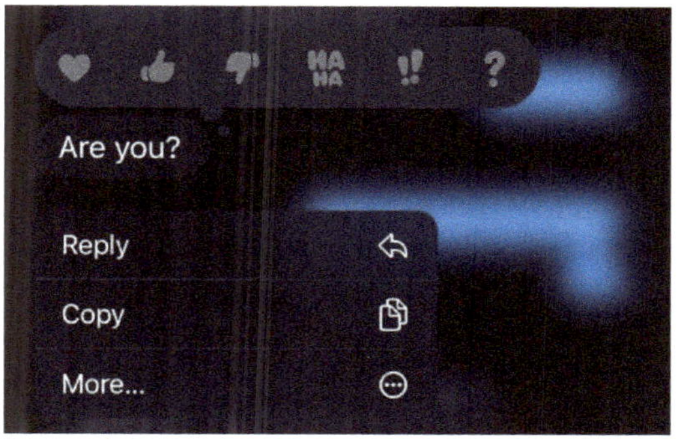

Once you tap Reply, you just reply as you normally would.

This is going to alert the person and they'll see the message with a reply notification under the message.

If it's several texts above, they'll also see it like the below message.

Pinning Messages

If you text a lot, then it might get a little cumbersome replying. The way Messages works is the most recent conversations go to the top. This mostly works well, but you can also pin favorites to the top.

In the example below, my wife is pinned to the top of the conversations. Even though other people have written me more recently, she will always be up there (unless I remove her). That makes it easy to reply.

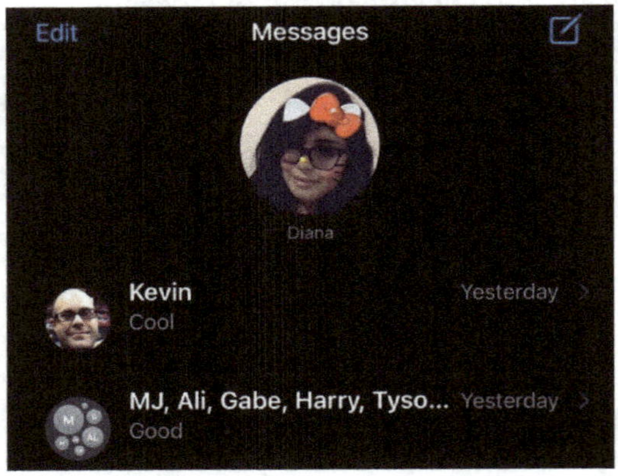

To add or remove someone from the top, tap the Edit button in the upper left corner, then select Edit Pins (or swipe right over their message).

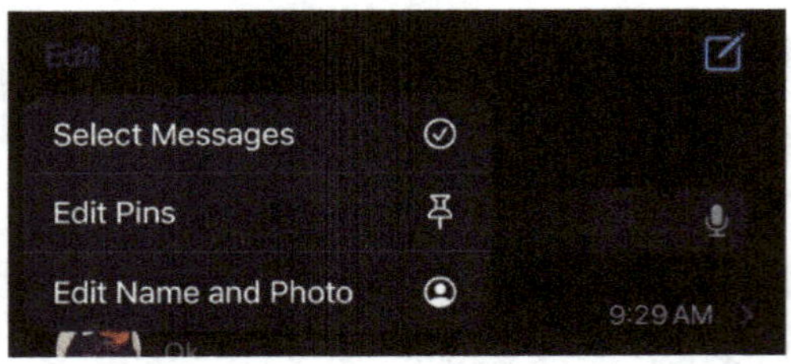

If you want to remove them, tap the minus icon above their photo (in the upper left corner); if you want to add them, tap the yellow pin icon.

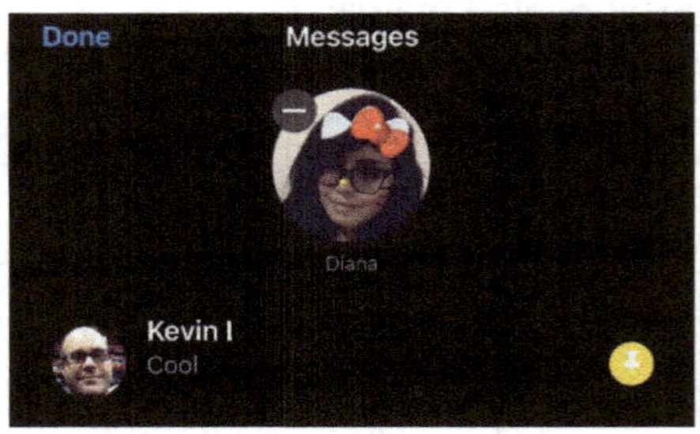

You can have several people pinned to the top. Personally, I find three is good, but you can add even more.

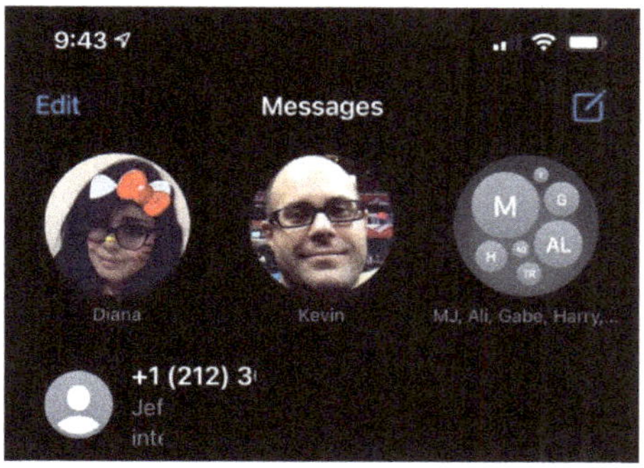

Photos In Messages

Messages will organize photos sent in groups of two or three vertically.

If you send more than three photos at one time, they will stack them together, and you can toggle through them by swiping over the photo left or right.

Unsend Messages

Let's be honest here: we've all sent text we've regretted. You can unsend or edit those text. Just tap and hold the message (you have to do this relatively quickly—if too much time passes, the option disappears), then select either Undo Send or Edit.

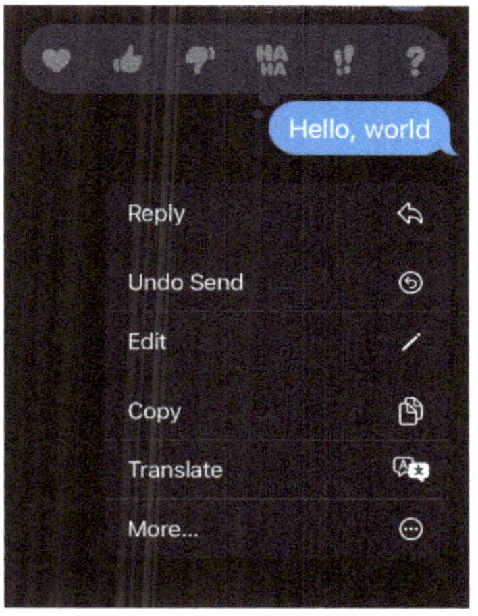

If you think this will get you out of the doghouse and you can say "I never said that!" Think again! The person on the other end of the text will see that the message has been unsent or edited.

Notifications

When you have your tablet locked, you'll start seeing notifications at some point; this tells you things like "You have a new email," "Don't forget to set your alarm," etc.

So, when you see all your notifications on your lock screen, they'll be organized by what they are. To see all the notifications from any one category, just tap it.

Not a fan of grouping? No problem. You can turn it off for any app. Head to Settings, then Notifications, then tap the app you want to turn grouping off for. Under Notification Groupings, just turn off automatic.

Using AirDrop

AirDrop was introduced in iOS 7, though Apple fans have likely used the Mac OS version on MacBooks and iMacs. In Mac OSX Sierra and Yosemite, you'll finally be able to share between iPadOS and your Mac using AirDrop.

AirDrop is Apple's file sharing service, and it comes standard on iPadOS 15 devices. You can activate AirDrop from the Share icon anywhere in iPadOS 15. If other AirDrop users are nearby, you'll see anything they're sharing in AirDrop, and they can see anything you share.

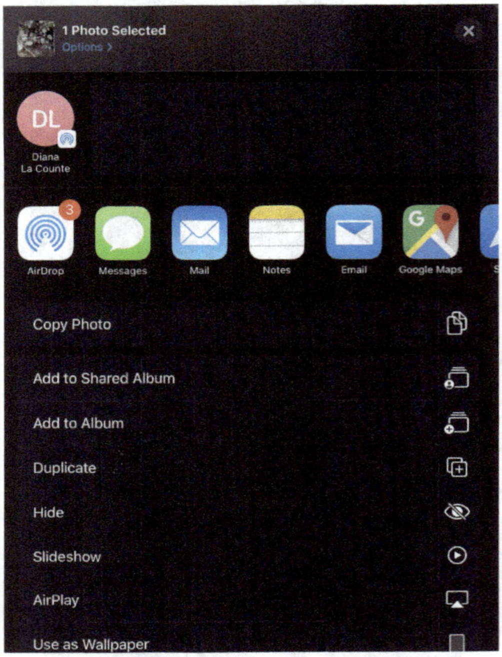

Multitasking

Multitasking is the ability to have more than two apps running at the same time.

When you have a single app running, notice those three dots? That's your multitask menu. It's there whether or not you are using the feature. Tap it and it expands to show you can either switch from multitask to full screen, have two apps side by side, or have a slide over multitask window (where one appears over the other).

When you are using multitask and you click that menu, watch what happens on the bottom: there's a multitask window previewed. This let you quickly toggle between multitask apps.

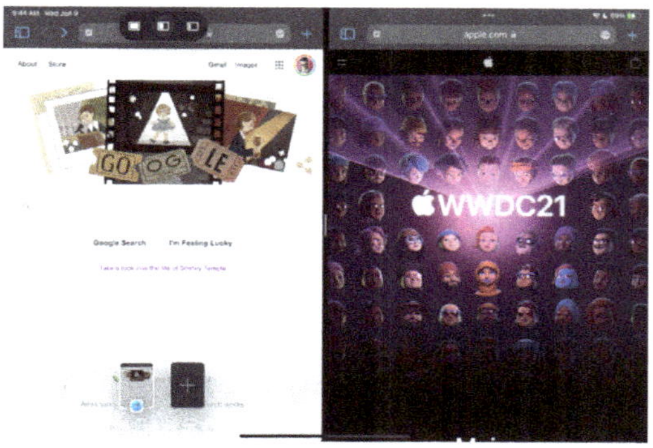

In the example below, I have two multitask windows I can toggle between. If I want to add a new one, I tap New Window.

To close windows, just swipe up over the thumbnail you want to close.

Stage Manager

Stage manager is a way to multitask between apps. Typically you have one app open; when you want to get to the next app, you have to get out of the app, find the app, and open it.

With Stage Manager turned on, it looks like the image below.

The thumbnails let you quickly toggle between the apps that you have open.

Go to the control center in the upper right corner of your screen to turn it on.

Press it again to turn it off. When you press it again, it will also give you the option for how you'd like to sort apps.

You can also use it horizontally.

Picture in Picture

As a video plays (or during a FaceTime video call), press the Home button and the video scales down to a corner of your display. You can also pinch it with three fingers to shrink it.

Once it's shrunk, you can move it around your screen to any of the four corners.

If you want to close the video, tap the 'x'; if you want to enlarge it, tap the far-left button; and if you want to play it within another app, just open any app.

Chapter 4: More of the Basics

Mail

The iPad mini lets you add multiple email addresses from virtually any email client you can think of. Yahoo, Gmail, AOL, Exchange, Hotmail, and many more can be added to your iPad mini so that you will be able to check your email no matter where you are. To add an email address, click on the Settings app icon, then scroll to the middle where you'll see Mail, Contacts & Calendar. You will then see logos for the biggest email providers, but if you have another type of email just click on Other and continue.

If you don't know your email settings, you will need to visit the Mail Settings Lookup page on the Apple website. There you can type in your entire email address, and the website will show you what information to type and where in order to get your email account working on the tablet. The settings change with everyone, so what works for one provider may not work with another. Once you are finished adding as many email accounts as you may need, you will be able to click on the Mail app icon on your tablet's Home screen and view each inbox separately, or all at once.

Unsend Message

If you sent a message by mistake, you can unsend it…kind of. The caveat here is you have to unsend it within ten seconds. So, this isn't to unsend that horrible message to your boss that you put out last week and now regret! The goal is just to unsend things you sent by mistake—like you forgot to attach something.

To use it, tap the blue button at the bottom of your inbox that appears after sending it. Don't see it? Unfortunately, that means your window has passed and it's too late. If you manage to do it in time, the email will go back to the compose state.

Schedule Mail

There are probably a lot of times that you want to draft an email, but not send it right away. When I teach classes, I will schedule emails to go out on the day of the class, for example; that way they're ready to go and are automatically triggered the day of the class.

To do this, compose the email as you normally would, but instead of tapping the blue arrow to send, long press it (i.e. hold it down); that will bring up an option that asks when you want to send it. Make your pick, then tap Done.

Email Reminder

If you want to be reminded about an email later in the week, then open the email and select the reply button. This will bring up several options. One is Remind me.

Surfing the Internet with Safari

You've already seen how the address bar works. To search for something, you use the same exact box. That's how you can search for anything on the Internet. Think of it like a Google, Bing, or Yahoo! search engine in the corner of your screen. In fact, that's exactly what it is. Because when you search, it will use one of those search engines to find results.

If you've used Safari before, it's probably going to look a little different for you. In 2021, Apple gave Safari a facelift to make it even more resourceful. It's great on the iPad, but even better when you have an entire ecosystem of devices.

Let's dig into the anatomy of the browser, then I'll break down how it works.

The top toolbar looks pretty bare. Looks can be deceiving because there's a lot here. Starting on the far left is the side menu button, which brings up your Saved Tabs (more on that later), private viewing mode, history and more; the middle is where you can either type or search for the website (the microphone lets you say it instead of type it), and finally the Plus button lets you open a new tab.

Tabs don't look like tabs on the iPad. In the example below, there are three opened tabs. The middle one is the opened website, the smaller two (Start Page and Amazon) are the opened, non-active, tabs.

There are a few ways to close a tab. One is to tap the X next to the website name (this is only on the active tab); the other way is the tap and hold your finger on the tab, then select tab; and the last way is to tap and hold the Plus button, then selecting to close the tab.

When you tap and hold over the Plus button, you'll see a few other options as well. One is Open New Window; this will open a new Safari multitask window next to the current window—so you have two browsers opened at the same time. There's also an option for a New Private Tab; this is to search the web without having your history saved—it's great for gift shopping if you share a device.

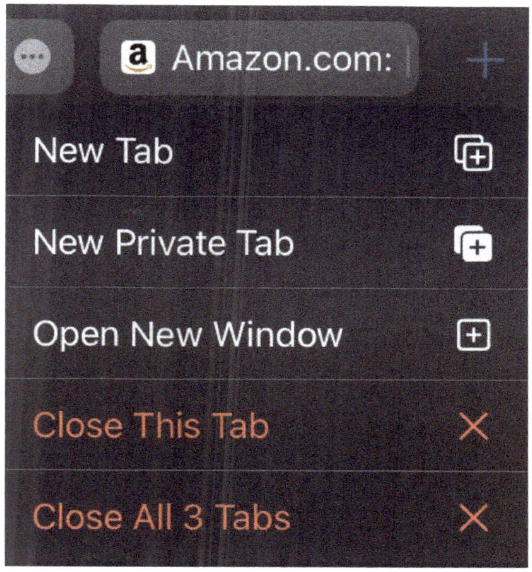

Website Options

When you click the three dots on the page you are currently visiting, you'll get several more options. This is where you'll go if you want to add the page to your Bookmarks or add it to your Favorites (Favorites show up whenever you start Safari when it's been closed—it's known as your "Start Page.") You can also share the page with someone, change the text size, and see a Privacy Report. Privacy Report shows all the trackers on a page, so you know what information a company is collecting about you.

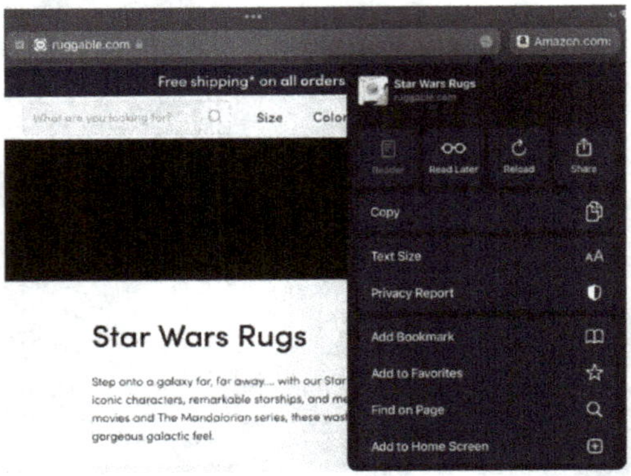

Menu Options

On the far left side is the option to bring up the menu pane. The menu can be shown as you browse, or you can collapse it once you pull up what you are looking for.

There's a few things you can do here. First is Group Tabs; there's a lot to Group Tabs, so I'll go over it in the next section. Start Page is your homepage; Private turns your browser into a private web surfing experiences where your web history and passwords aren't saved.

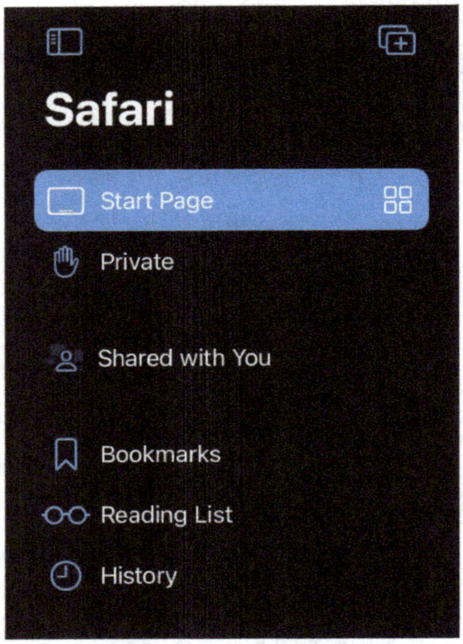

Shared With You

Shared With You is where you'll see things that have been shared recently. As an example: my wife and I share a lot of links through text. When she sends one, they'll automatically show up here. That way, I don't have to search through dozens of texts to find the page she mentioned—it's already been saved.

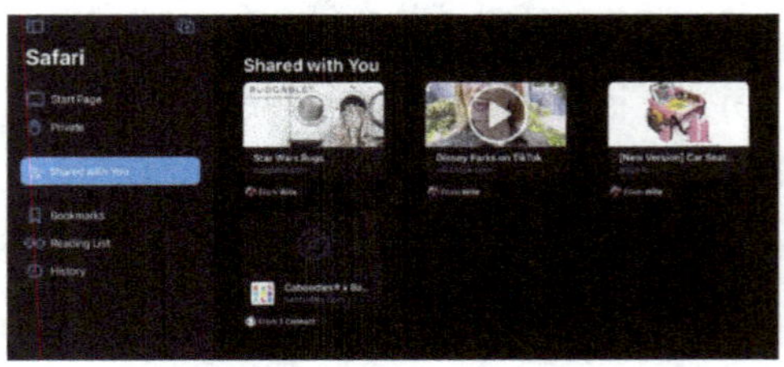

If you want to remove the link, then tap and hold your finger on the page preview. This brings up several options—one is remove. You can also use the options here to reply to the message, open in the background or copy the link.

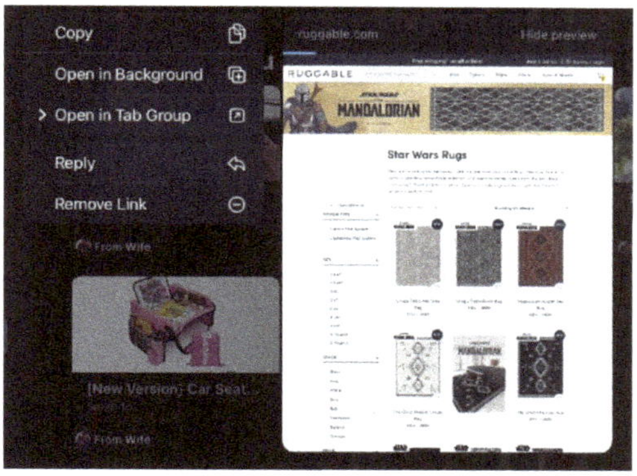

Safari Bookmarks

Below Shared With You are the Bookmarks; Bookmarks are pages you save because you regularly go to them. When you start getting a lot of Bookmarks, it's a good idea to put them into organized folders.

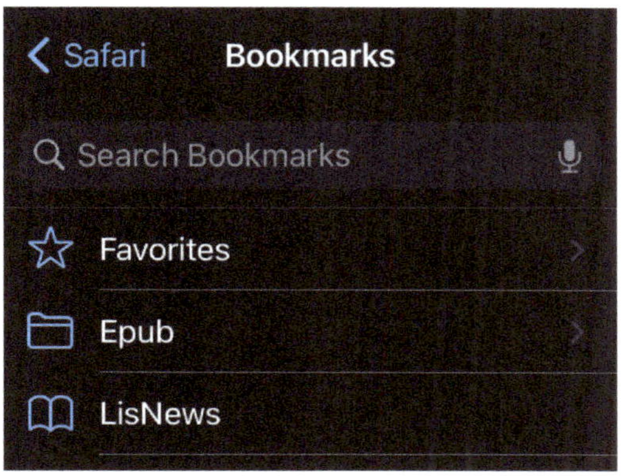

To create a folder, just go to the bottom of the page to Edit, then select New Folder. When you have selected Edit, you can also delete Bookmarks and move them into folders.

You can put folders into folders when you create them.

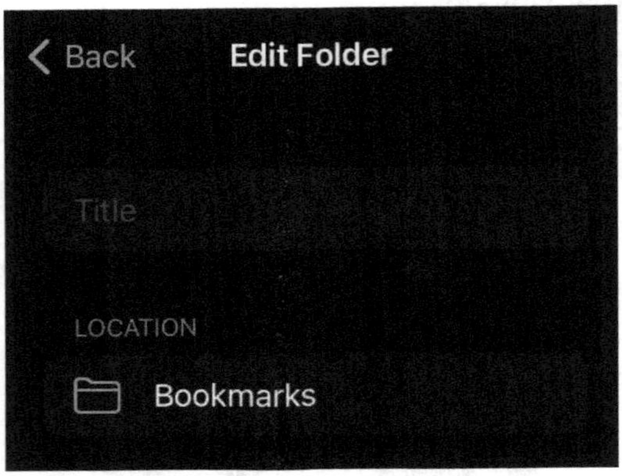

Web History

If you are not using Private mode, then all your history is saved; this is helpful if you ever forget a website you went to, but you know what day you went to it. If you ever want to clear your history, just tap the Clear option at the bottom of the page when you are viewing your history.

Tab Group

Tabs can be your best friend. Tab Group is the evolution of this friend. Tab Groups are kind of a combination of bookmarks and tabs. You basically save all your tabs into a group. So, for example, you can have a group called "Shopping" and when you click it, like magic, all your favorite shopping websites open into tabs.

To get started, open all the tabs that you want to be in your group, then go to the left menu, and click on the + button from the side menu and select New Empty Tab Group.

Type in the name of your group. Remember to be descriptive, so you know what your Tab Group is for.

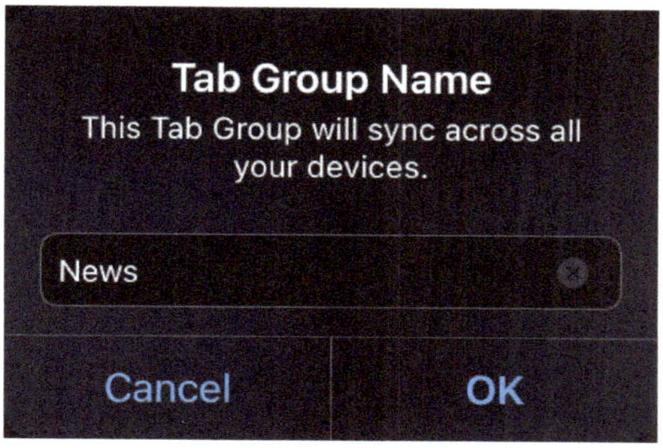

All the tabs are now saved in your group; in the example below, there are two tab groups; when I toggle between them, new tabs will open.

You can make changes to your group by tapping and holding on it.

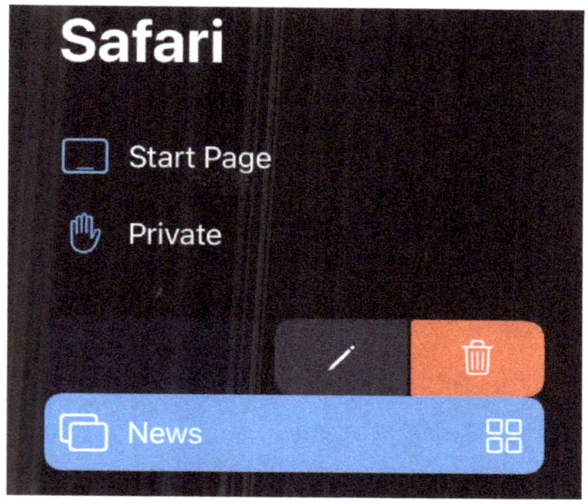

If you want a new tab to show there, just open up the tab while in that group and it will automatically be saved in the group.

Set Your Default Email / Web Browser

For a number of years, you were able to use other Mail and Web browsers in iOS, but you could not set it as a default. This changed in iOS 14...kind of. You can now have alternative default browsers and email clients, but the app has to be updated.

It's the developers (not Apple's) responsibility to update the app to take advantage of this feature; so when you try and change it using the steps below, and you don't see your preferred app, it's probably because either they haven't updated the app yet or you haven't updated the app yet (go to the App Store and make sure there's not an update for the app).

To change your preferred app, go to the Settings app. Next, go to the app you want to make the default (I'm using the Chrome browser in the example below); next, tap Default Browser.

Finally, check off your preferred browser. It saves automatically.

iTunes

The iTunes app found on your Home screen opens the biggest digital music store in the world. You will be able to purchase and download not just music, but also countless movies, TV shows, audiobooks, and more. On the iTunes home page, you can also find a What's Hot section, collections of music, and new releases.

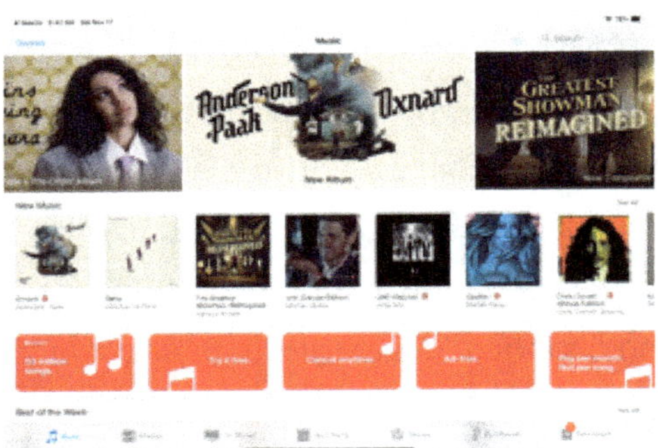

At the top, you will see the option to view either featured media or browse through the top charts. On the upper left corner is the Genres button. Clicking Genres will bring up many different types of music to help refine your search.

Apple Music

Apple Music is a relatively new service from Apple that gives you the ability to stream the entire iTunes store and receive curated playlists from music experts tailored to your preferences. It costs $9.99 a month, but you can take advantage of the three-month free trial to see if this service is for you before paying for it. It also offers discount subscription pricing for family plans and college students.

Buying Apps

So how do you buy, download and finally remove apps? I'll look at that in this section.

To purchase apps, and I don't actually mean paying for them because you can purchase a free app without paying for it, follow the following:

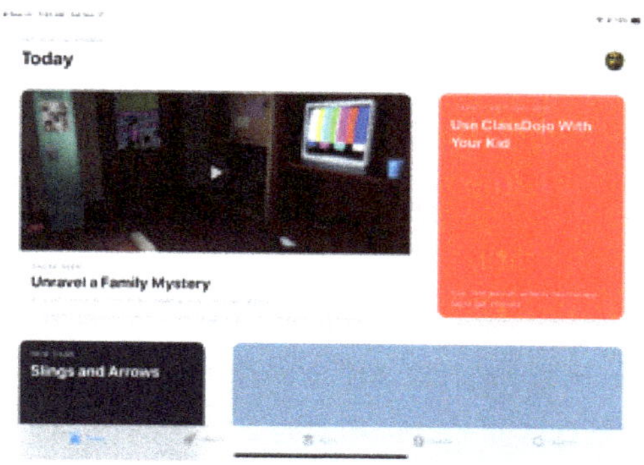

The first thing you see when you open the App Store are the featured apps. This is to say games, lots and lots of games! Games are the top selling category in the App Store, but don't worry, there is more there than just games. Later in this handbook, I will tell you some of the essential apps you should get, but for now, let's see how the App Store works so that you discover some of them yourself.

If you hear about a new app and want to check it out, use the Search option.

When you find an app you want to buy, simply tap the price button and type in your App Store password. Remember that just because an app is free to download doesn't mean you won't have to pay something to use it. Many apps use 'in-app purchases' which means that you have to buy something within the app. You will be notified before you purchase anything though.

Apps are constantly coming out with updates like new, better features. Updates are almost always free, unless noted, and are easy to install. Just click on the last tab: Updates. If you have an app that needs to be updated, you will see it here. You will also see what's new in the app. If you see one, tap Update to begin the update.

If you bought an app, but accidentally deleted it, or changed your mind about deleting it, don't worry! You can download the app again in the same place that you see the updates. Just tap on Purchased.

When you tap the Purchased button, you will see two options: one is to see all the apps you have purchased and one to just see the apps that you have purchased but are not on your iPad mini. Tap the one that says Not on This iPad to re-download anything, at no cost. Just tap the Cloud button to the right of the screen. You can even download it again if you bought it on another iPad as long as it's under the same account.

Deleting apps is easy; on your Home screen, tap and hold the icon of the app you want to remove, then tap the 'x' on top of the app.

Calendar

Among the other pre-installed apps that came with your new iPad mini, perhaps one of the most used apps you'll encounter is the Calendar. You can switch between viewing appointments, tasks, or everything laid out in a one day, one week, or one month view.

Combine your calendar with email accounts or iCloud to keep your appointments and tasks synced across all of your devices, and never miss another appointment.

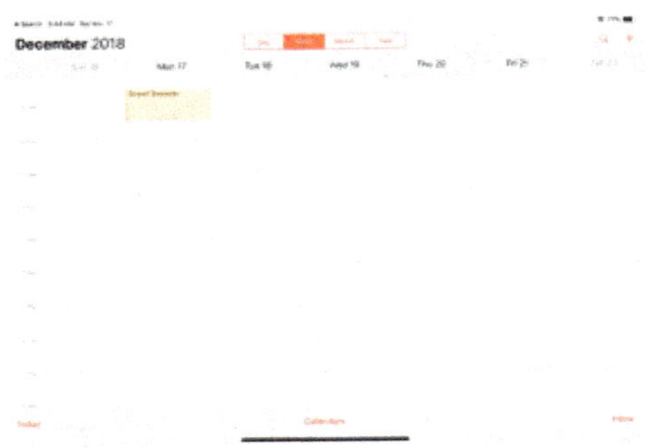

Creating an Appointment

To create an appointment, click on the Calendar icon on your Home screen. Click on whichever day you would like to set the appointment for, and then tap the '+' button in the corner. Here you will be able to name and edit your event, as well as connect it to an email or iCloud account in order to allow for syncing.

When editing your event, pay special attention to the duration of your event. Select the start and end times, or choose "All Day" if it's an all-day event. You will also have a chance to set it as a recurring event by clicking on Repeat and selecting how often you want it to repeat. In the case of a bill or car payment, for example, you could either select Monthly (on this day) or every 30 days, which are two different things. After you select your repetition, you can also choose how long you'd like for that event to repeat itself: for just one month, a year, forever, and everything in between.

Maps

The Maps app is back and better than ever. After Apple parted ways with Google Maps several years ago, Apple decided to develop its own, made-for-iPad map and navigation system. The result is a beautiful travel guide that takes full advantage of the newest iPad mini resolutions. Full screen mode allows every corner of the tablet to be filled with the app, and there's an automatic night mode. You'll be able to search for places, restaurants, gas stations, concert halls, and other venues near you at any time, and turn-by-turn navigation is available for walking, biking, cycling, driving, or commuting. Traffic is updated in real time, so if an accident occurs ahead of you or there is construction going on, Maps will offer a faster alternative and warn you of the potential traffic jam.

The turn-by-turn navigation is easy to understand without being distracting, and the 3D view makes potentially difficult scenarios (like highway exits that come up abruptly) much more pleasant. Another convenient feature is the ability to avoid highways and toll roads entirely.

To set up navigation, tap on the Maps icon. On the bottom of the screen is a search for place or address; for homes you need an address, but businesses just need a name. Click on it and enter your destination once prompted.

When you find your destination's address, click on Route, and choose between walking or driving directions. For businesses, you also have the option of reading reviews and calling the company directly.

For hands-free navigation, just say "Hey Siri" and say "Navigate to" or "Take me to" followed by the address or name of the location that you'd like to go to.

If you'd like to avoid highways or tolls, simply tap the More Options button and select the option that you want.

Apple Maps also lets you see a 3D view of thousands of locations. To enable this option, tap the 'i' in the upper right corner. After this, select satellite view.

If 3D view is available, you'll notice a change immediately. You can use two fingers to make your map more or less flat. You can also select 2D to remove 3D altogether.

Maps has taken big strides to compete against Google; in 2019, it added in a street level view to major cities like New York and Los Angeles with more expected soon. When you tap and hold on a location, you might notice it as an available view (if you don't see it, then it's not in that city yet).

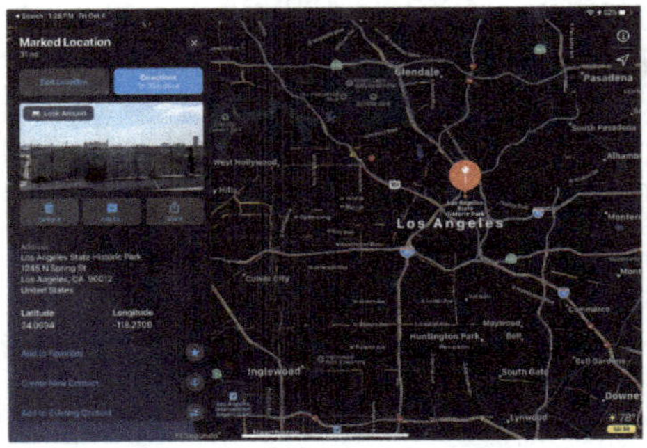

When you tap on the view, then it gets larger.

Finally, similar to the iPhone version of Maps, iPad lets you add locations into collections so you can organize all of your favorite spots.

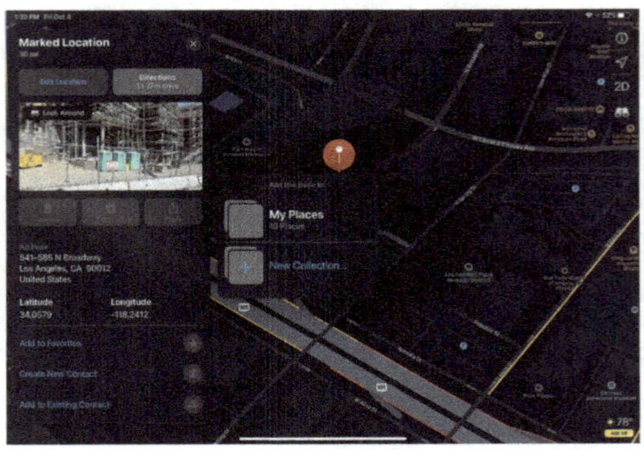

Maps got a small upgrade with what is shown in iPadOS and iOS 15, but it still functions largely the same.

The biggest difference with the OS 15 update is buildings now have more shape. So, in the example below of an amusement park, you can see the shape of the castle and mountain. This is only available in some regions.

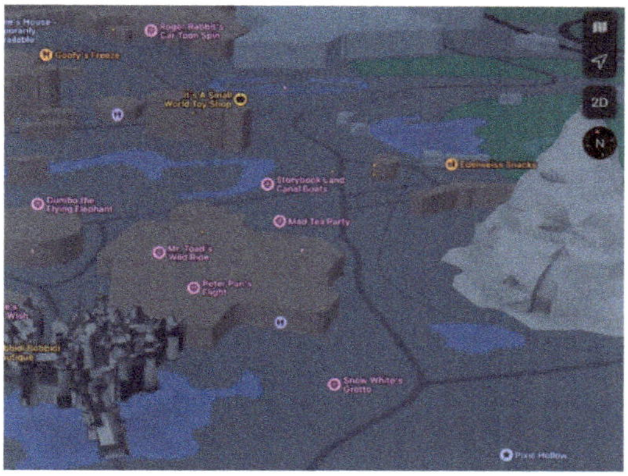

Some, but not all, cities also have more in terms of lanes on the road; if the city has been configured, you'll be able to see more details on lanes to help you navigate through the city and know what lanes to be in. If you don't see this detail, it's because the city has not been set up yet.

Maps (Multiple Stops)

Getting directions is nice, but you probably often like to make a few stops along the way. You can add multiple stops if that's the case.

Let's say I want to figure out how to get my kid to an amusement park from the location I'm staying. I type in the name of the park, then tap directions.

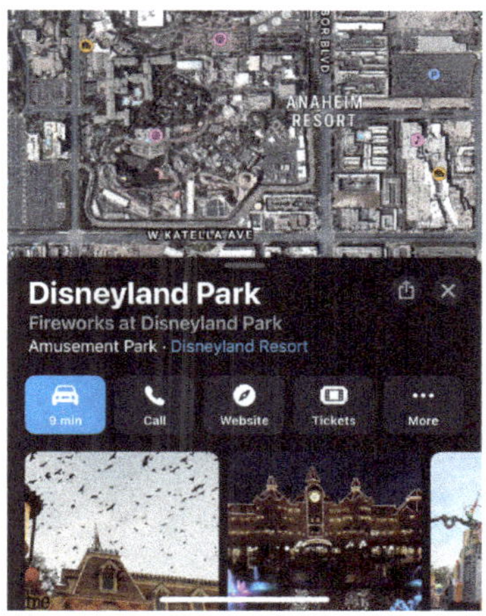

Easy, peasy, right! But, oh, no! I just got in the car and I'm out of gas! That's no problem with maps. I just tap the Add Stop button.

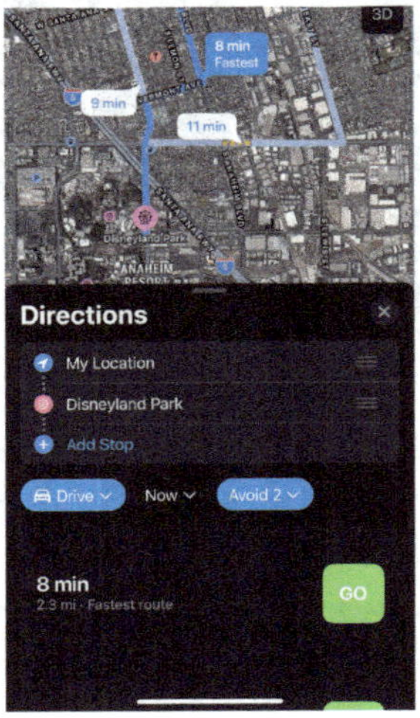

Next, I type in the address, or, in this case, just type in "Gas." That's going to give me all the nearby gas stations. When I see the one I want, I just tap Add.

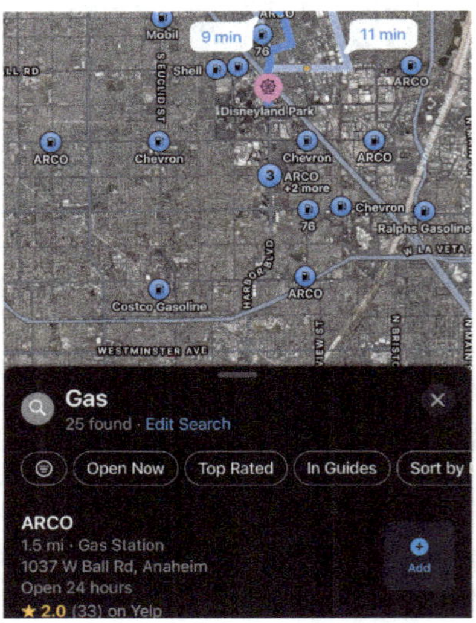

Now the stop has been added into the directions–but with a caveat: it's added to the end. You can easily move the order of stops, however, by tapping and holding on the three lines to the right of the stop, then dragging it up or down to the order you want it.

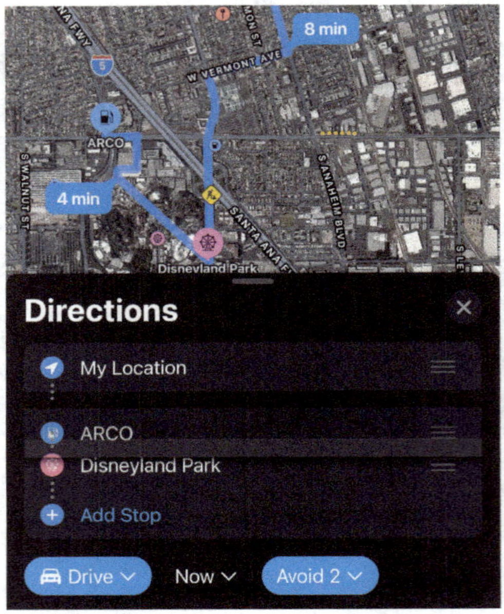

What if the kids are also saying they're hungry?! You don't want to pay amusement park prices for breakfast, do you?! Just tap Add Stop again. Now I have a map to get to the donut place, a gas station, and finally the amusement park.

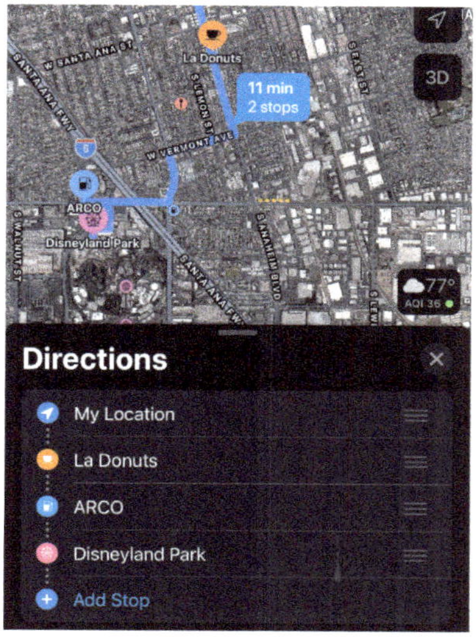

Map Guides

Map Guides are only available in larger cities. When you search for a city in the Map app, you will see the guides right under the directions button. You can also share the guide or save it.

As you look at the guides, it will show you recommendations on the map, and you can save them for later.

Find My

If you used Find My Phone or Find My Friend on previous OSes, then shocker: they're gone! These two powerful apps let you see where your friends were on a map or where your devices were on a map.

They're essentially the same app with a different purpose; so instead of keeping both, Apple decided to delete them and combine them into one app called Find My.

The app is pretty simple. Three tabs on the bottom. One to find your friends (i.e. People), one to find your devices, and one to change settings (i.e. Me).

If you want to see where your friend is at, ask them to share their location with you in the People section.

It's not very helpful using an app to find your iPad if you don't have your iPad. If that's the case, you can also use your computer browser to see it at iCloud.com.

Quick Notes

Quick Notes is a very easy to use feature for jotting down notes. How easy? Swipe up from the lower right corner of your screen. That's it!

Well, that's kind of it—you have to click a Get Started button the first time you try it.

After that first open, a pop up note will always appear when you swipe up from that lower right corner. It floats above other windows, so you can jot down notes as you are on a website or any other app. Once you have written the note, tap the Done button in the upper left corner of the opened note. It saves it automatically and also syncs it.

Notes

The Notes app has always been the go-to app for jotting down quick and simple notes—it's like Word or Pages, but without all the fancy stuff. In iPadOS, Notes is still simple—but it got a whole lot fancier…while retaining the simplicity that people love about it.

At first glance, Notes looks basically the same as it always has. Notice that little plus sign above the keyboard? That's what's different.

Tap the '+' button one time, and you'll see the options that have been added.

Starting from the left side is a checkmark, which is what you press if you'd like to make a checklist instead of a note. For each new checkmark, just tap the return button on the keyboard.

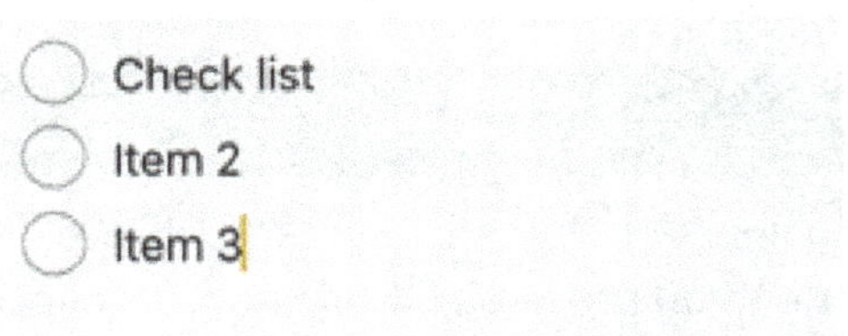

The 'Aa' button is what you would press if you would like to format the note a little (larger fonts, bold, bulleted text, etc.).

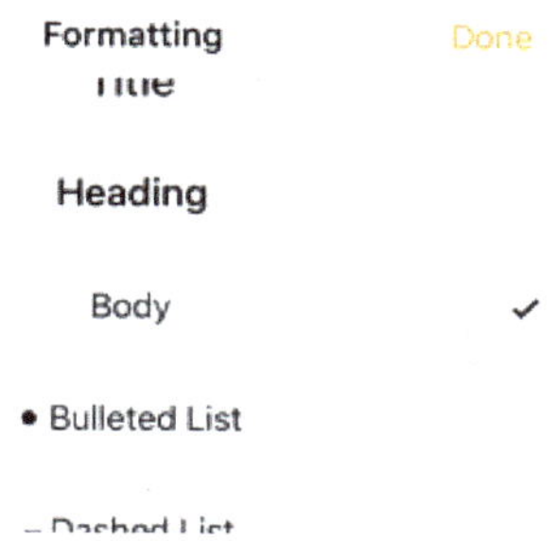

The little camera button will let you add a photo you have taken or let you take a photo from within the app and insert it.

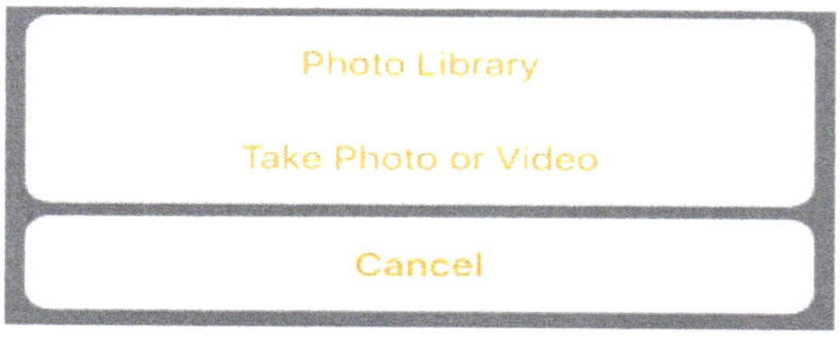

And finally, the squiggly line lets you draw in the Notes app; when you press it, you'll see three different brushes (pen, marker, and pencil) that each work a little differently, as well as a ruler and eraser.

There's also a round black circle—tapping that lets you change the color of the brush.

Just tap the Done button in the upper right corner once you've picked your color and it will be changed.

Once you tap the Done button after you've finished drawing, you will go back to the note. If you tap the drawing, however, it will activate it again and you can make changes or add to your drawing.

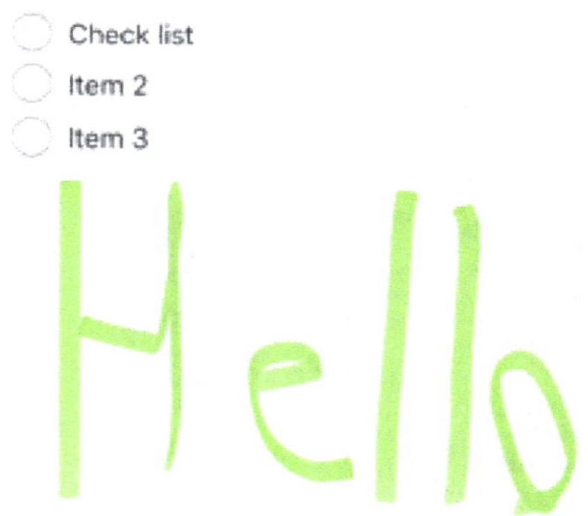

It's obviously not the most advance drawing app—but that's the point—it's not supposed to be. As the name of the app says, this app is just for jotting or drawing quick notes.

In the Settings menu a Search option has been added at the top. There are a lot of Settings in iOS and there are more and more with each update—Search Settings let you quickly access the setting you want. So, for instance, if you want to stop getting notifications for a certain app, you no longer have to thumb through endless apps—now just search for it.

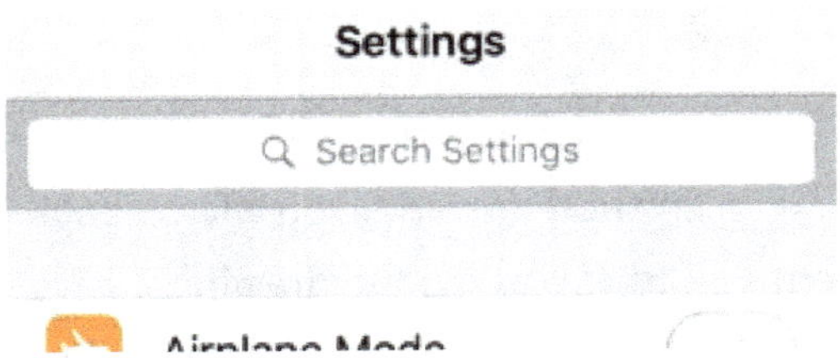

Notes has also been added to Safari, so if you want to add a website to a note, it's now possible.

Whenever you see the option to use Markup you will be using Notes interface.

Search Text in App

When you swipe down from the middle of the screen, you can quickly search for apps, which is helpful if you have a lot of them. You can also search for text within apps by scrolling down to the section titled "Search in Apps."

Universal Control

Some people like to really invest in the Apple ecosystem—and who can blame them? They make great products. So they might have an iMac, MacBook, and iPad. Apple understands these users and has created a feature called Universal Control. Universal Control lets you share things (from files and images to keyboards and trackpads) easily. What does that mean? Let's pretend you have a MacBook and iPad Mini. When enabled, you can open Pages on your iPad, and drag an image from your MacBook to your iPad Mini. You can also share your MacBook's trackpad and keyboard with your iPad.

Using it is pretty simple. Put your iPad next to your MacBook and make sure they are on the same wireless network and have Bluetooth on—or connect the iPad to the MacBook with a USB-C then drag your mouse to the edge of the screen to move it onto your iPad screen. It's all pretty intuitive. Both devices also need to be running the latest version of MacOS (OS Monterey) and iPadOS (OS15). If you are reading this book at the publication date, that's bad news for you because MacOS Monterey is not quite out as of this writing. It also might not launch with the first OS update. It is expected in the fall.

If you want to prepare for it, then you just need to set up a couple of things. First, on your MacBook or iMac, go to the Apple Menu in the upper left corner, then select System Preference, and finally go to General. In the General menu check off Allow Handoff between this Mac and your iCloud devices. Next, on your iPad, go to the Settings app, then general; next, turn on AirPlay & Handoff if it is toggled off.

Focus

Do Not Disturb has been on iPads for several updates, but Focus is a new addition. Focus works in a way that's very similar to Do Not Disturb, but it's more customizable. The idea is to create different Focus groups—for example, you can set it to Work and only colleagues can get ahold of you, not friends.

To start or create a Focus session, swipe down from the upper right corner. This brings up the Control Panel; tap on the Focus option.

It will ask you what kind of Focus you want to start. If you have never created a Focus, tap Get Started on the type you want to create, or click the + New Focus to create a custom one.

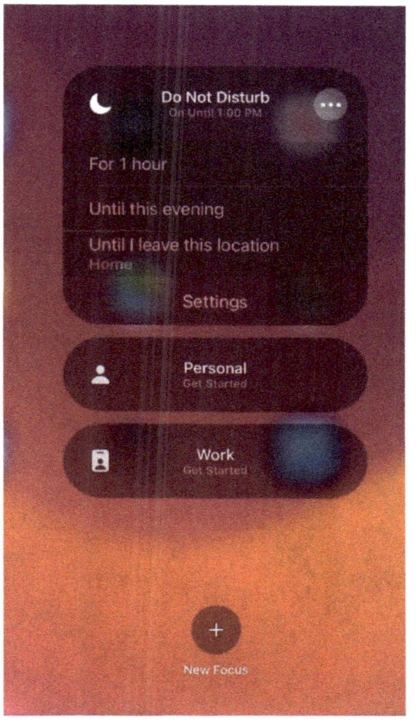

Creating a New Focus will bring up a few suggestions for types of Focus groups you can create.

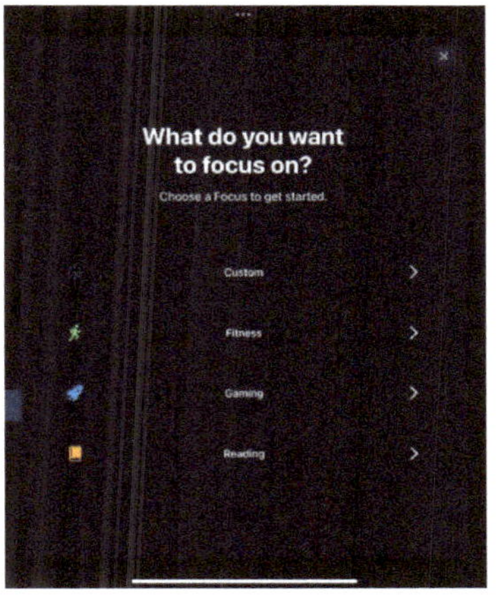

Click on any of the arrows and you can set who can contact you, what kind of apps are allowed, and even the hours you want it to automatically go on at. For example, you can say turn the Reading Focus on every night at 10:00 p.m.

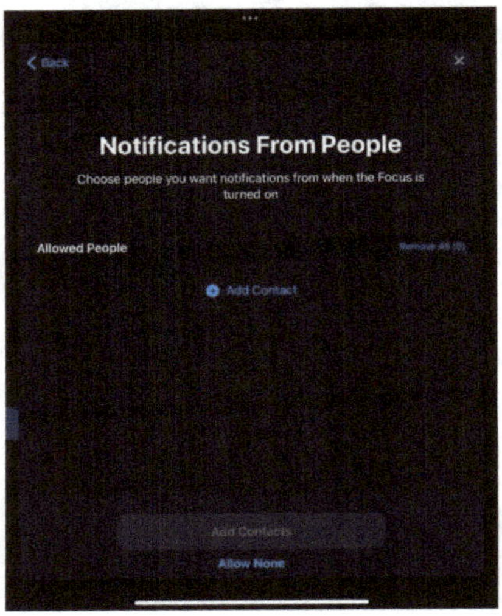

The custom Focus works the same way, but you have to give it a name and icon.

You can go into your System Settings at any time to make edits to your Focus groups.

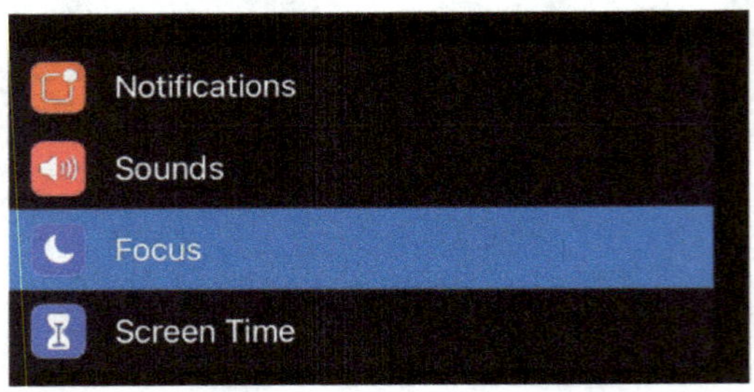

In the edit menu, you'll be able to change when it's active, what people can contact you and what apps are enabled.

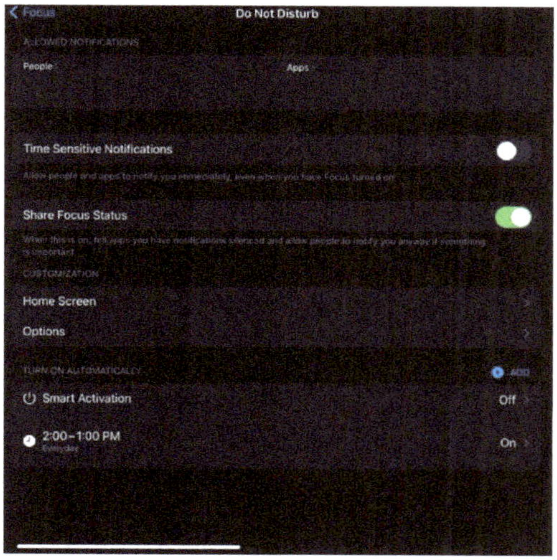

Weather App

The weather app has been around for years, but iPadOS 16 gave it some big enhancements. It's no longer just an app to get the weather. It's an app to get precise details about the weather.

When you click on a specific day, it will give you an hourly forecast, so you can plan your day.

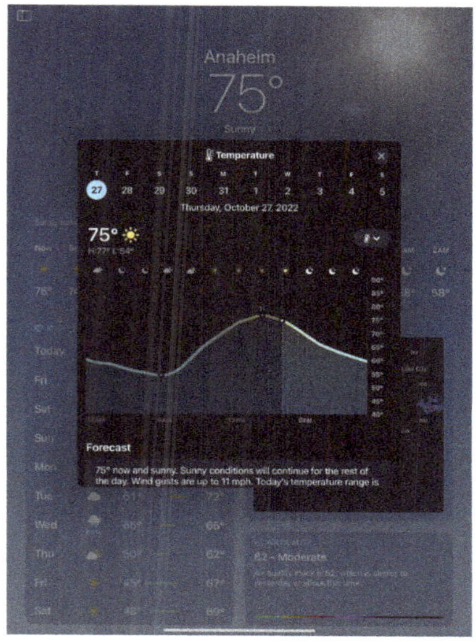

The Colorful Guide to the 2022 iPad and iPad Pro

CHAPTER 5: GET CUSTOMIZED

Now that you know your way around, it's time to dig into the settings and make this tablet completely custom to you!

For most of this chapter, I'll be hanging out in the Settings area, so if you aren't already there, tap Settings from your Home screen.

SCREEN TIME

To use Screen Time, head on into Settings > Screen Time

You can click on any app to see how much time you've spent in it, and even what your average is. From here you can also add limits.

DO NOT DISTURB MODE

Do Not Disturb mode is a handy feature located near the top of your Settings app. When this operational mode is enabled, you won't receive any notifications and all of your calls will be silenced. This is a useful trick for those times when you can't afford to be distracted (and let's face it, your iPad is as communicative as they come, and sometimes you'll need to have some peace and quiet!). Clock alarms will still sound.

To turn on, schedule and customize Do Not Disturb, just tap on Do Not Disturb in Settings. You can schedule automatic times to activate this feature, like your work hours, for example. You can also specify certain callers who should be allowed when your tablet is set to Do Not Disturb. This way, your mother can still get through, but you won't have to hear every incoming email. To do this, use the Allow Call From command in Do Not Disturb settings.

Do Not Disturb is also accessible through the Control Center (swipe down from the upper right corner of the screen to access it at any time).

Notifications and Widgets

Notifications are one of the most useful features on the iPad, but chances are you won't need to be informed of every single event that's set as a default in your Notifications Center. To adjust Notifications preferences, go to Settings > Notifications.

By tapping the app, you can turn Notifications off or on and finesse the type of notification from each app. It's a good idea to whittle this list down to the apps that you truly want to be notified from—for example, if you're not an investor, turn off Stocks! Reducing the number of sounds your iPad makes can also reduce tablet-related frazzledness. For example, in Mail, you may want your tablet to make a sound when you receive email from someone on your VIP list but to only display badges for other, less important email.

General Settings

The General menu item is a little bit of a catchall. This is where you'll find information about your iPad, including its current version of iOS and any available software updates. Fortunately, iPadOS 15 ushers in an era of smaller, more efficient updates, so you won't find yourself scrambling to delete apps in order to make space for the latest improvements. You can also check your tablet and iCloud storage here.

The Accessibility options are located here as well. You can set your iPad according to your needs with Zoom, Voiceover, large text, color adjustment, and more. There are a quite a few Accessibility options that can make iPadOS 15 easy for everyone to use, including Grayscale View and improved Zoom options.

A handy Accessibility option that's a little disguised is the AssistiveTouch setting. This gives you a menu that helps you access device-level functions. Enabling it brings up a floating menu designed to help users who have difficulty with screen gestures like swiping or with manipulating the iPad's physical buttons. Another feature for those with visual needs is Magnifier. Turning this on allows your camera to magnify things, and you can also click the Home button on older models and magnify anything that you're looking at.

I recommend taking some time and tapping through the General area, just so you know where everything is!

Sounds

Hate that vibration when your tablet rings? Want to change your ring tone? Head to the Sounds Settings menu! Here you can turn vibration on or off and assign ring tones to a number of iPad functions. I do suggest finding an isolated space before you start trying out all the different sound settings—it's fun, but possibly a major annoyance to those unlucky enough not to be playing with their own new iPad!

Tip: You can apply individual ringtones and message alerts to your contacts. Just go to the person's contact screen in Contacts, tap Edit, and tap Assign Ringtone.

Customizing Brightness and Wallpaper

On the iPad, wallpaper refers to the background image on your Home screen and to the image displayed when your iPad is locked (Lock screen). You can change either image using two methods.

For the first method, visit Settings > Wallpapers. You'll see a preview of your current wallpaper and Lock screen here. Tap Choose a New Wallpaper. From there, you can choose a pre-loaded dynamic (moving) or still image, or choose one of your own photos. Once you've chosen an image, you'll see a preview of the image as a Lock screen. Here, you can turn off Perspective Zoom (which makes the image appear to shift as you tilt your tablet) if you like. Tap Set to continue. Then choose whether to set the image as the Lock screen, Home screen, or both.

The other way to make the change is through your Photo app. Find the photo you'd like to set as a wallpaper image and tap the Share button. You'll be given a choice to set an image as a background, a Lock screen, or both.

If you want to use images from the web, it's fairly easy. Just press and hold the image until the Save Image / Copy / Cancel message comes up. Saving the image will save it to your Recently Added photos in the Photos app.

Privacy

The Privacy heading in Settings lets you know what apps are doing with your data. Every app you've allowed to use Location Services will show up under Location Services (and you can toggle Location Services off and on for individual apps or for your whole device here as well). You can also go through your apps to check what information each one is receiving and transmitting.

When you are using any app that is using either the camera or microphone, you will now see a green indicator just above your cellular signal bar.

Compromised Password

Data breaches are pretty common these days; Apple is doing its part to be transparent about when they happen and help you fix it before it's a problem.

Go to the Settings app, then scroll until you get to Passwords.

Within this area (which is password protected) you can see all your stored passwords, but under Security Recommendations, you can also see if your password "may" have been compromised. I say "may" because this does not mean you have been hacked. It just means some data from a company was taken, and you might be on that list because you've had an account there in the past.

When you click the recommendations, it will take you one by one to each possible breach and show you why it's making the recommendation. In the example below, it says Apple had a breach and they are suggesting I change my password.

I can tap the Change Password on Website to change the password, or I can click the message to read a little more about it. In the example below, it's saying that it noticed I used the same password on another website, so I should change that one as well.

Privacy Report

In Safari, you can tap the AA icon next to the web address to see a Privacy Report.

The Privacy Report will tell me more about trackers that have been trying to follow me. A tracker is basically a little code embedded in a website to follow what I do. For example, it tells Facebook that I've visited a website about Legos, so it should start showing me Lego ads. Creepy, right?!

Mail, Contacts, Calendars Settings

If you need to add additional Mail, Contacts or Calendar accounts, tap Settings > Mail, Contacts and Calendars to do so. It's more or less the same process as adding a new account in-app. You can also adjust other settings here, including your email signature for each linked account. This is also a good place to check which aspects of each account are linked—for example, you may want to link your Tasks, Calendars and Mail from Exchange, but not your Contacts. You can manage all of this here.

There are a number of other useful settings here, including the frequency you want your accounts to check for mail (Push, the default, being the hardest on your battery life). You can also turn on features like Ask Before Deleting and adjust the day of the week you'd like your calendar to start on.

Adding Facebook and Twitter

If you use Twitter, Facebook or Flickr, you'll probably want to integrate them with your iPad. This is a snap to do. Just tap on Settings and look for Twitter, Facebook and Flickr in the main menu (you can also integrate Vimeo and Weibo accounts if you have them). Tap on the platform you want to integrate. From there, you'll enter your username and password. Doing this will allow you to share webpages, photos, notes, App Store pages, music and more, straight from your iPad's native apps.

iPad will ask you if you'd like to download the free Facebook, Twitter and Flickr apps when you configure your accounts if you haven't already done so. I recommend doing this—the apps are easy to use, free, and look great.

I have found that when I associated my Facebook account, my contacts list got extremely bloated. If you don't want to include your Facebook friends in your contacts list, adjust the list of applications that can access your Contacts in Settings > Facebook.

Family Sharing

Family Sharing is one of my favorite iPadOS 15 features. Family Sharing allows you to share App Store and iTunes purchases with family members (previously, accomplishing this required a tricky and not-entirely-in-compliance-with-terms-of-service dance). Turning on Family Sharing also creates a shared family calendar, photo album, and reminder list. Family members can also see each other's location in Apple's free Find My app and check the location of each other's devices. Overall, Family Sharing is a great way to keep everyone entertained and in sync! You can include up to six people in Family Sharing.

To enable Family Sharing, go to Settings > iCloud. Here, tap Set Up Family Sharing to get started. The person who initiates Family Sharing for a family is known as the family organizer. It's an important role, since every purchase made by family members will be made using the family organizer's credit card! Once you set up your family, they'll also be able to download your past purchases, including music, movies, books, and apps.

Invite your family members to join Family Sharing by entering their Apple IDs. As a parent, you can create Apple IDs for your children with parental consent. When you create a new child Apple ID, it is automatically added to Family Sharing.

There are two types of accounts in Family Sharing—adult and child. As you'd expect, child accounts have more potential restrictions than adult accounts do. Of special interest is the Ask to Buy option. This prevents younger family members from running up the family organizer's credit card bill by requiring parental authorization for purchases. The family organizer can also designate other adults in the family as capable of authorizing purchases on children's devices.

Creating Custom Shortcuts

If you want to put your own fresh spin on any icon, it's "technically" possible, but there are limitations. For example, you could change the iMessage icon to your wedding photo. What are the limitations? You will not get notification indicators on it. So your icon won't light up with a new message indicator, for example. It also launches through the Shortcuts app, which creates a delay for how quickly it opens.

To do this, you need to create a Shortcut for the app. If you don't see the Shortcuts app, then it's possible that you deleted it and need to install it again.

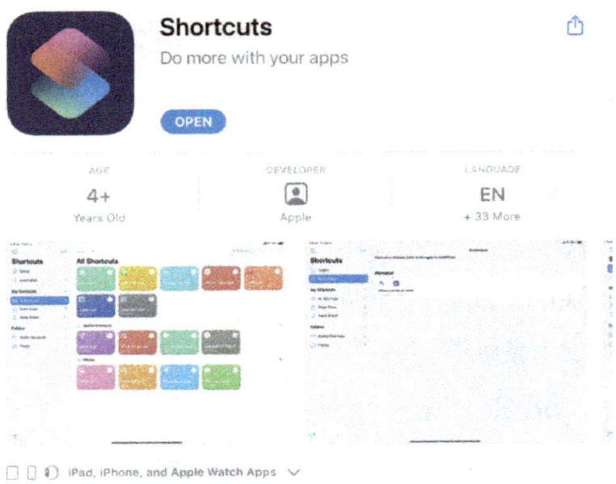

When the app launches, tap the + icon in the upper right corner.

Next, select Add Action.

You can search for all possible actions, but it's faster just to search for the actions you want to perform. In this case: Open app.

Tap Choose to select the app you want to open.

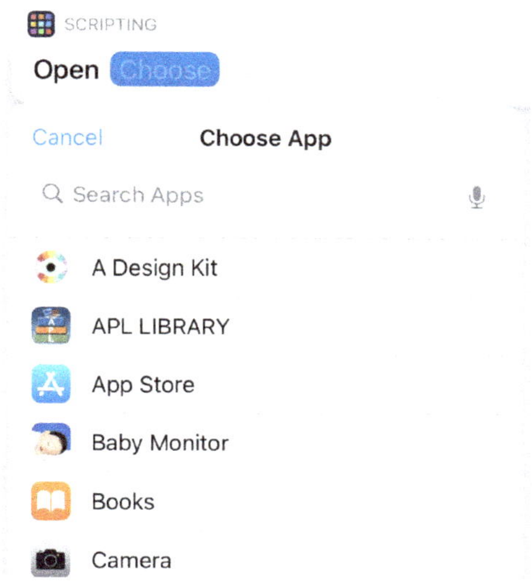

Type in the name of the app you want to open. I'm choosing the Messages app.

Next, tap the icon in the upper right corner with the three dots and blue circle.

You want to create an icon for it on your Home screen, so tap Add to Home Screen.

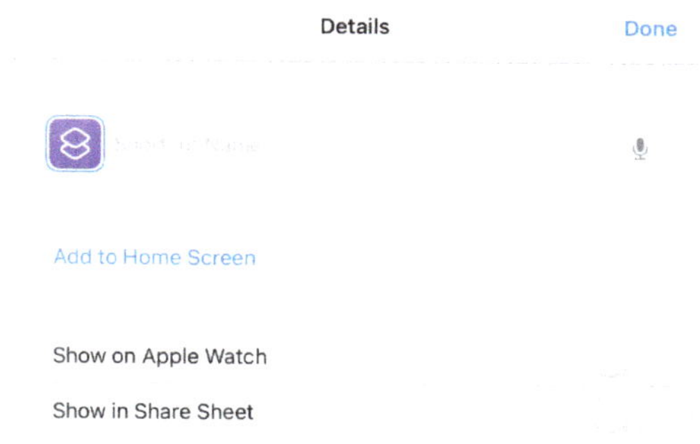

Tap the icon image, and select where the image is that you want to use, then select the image.

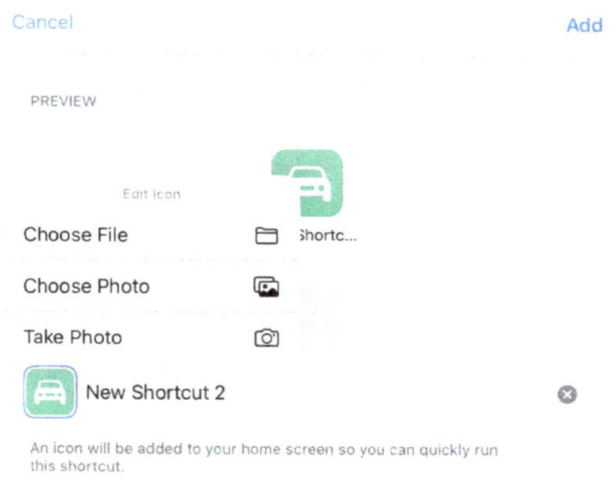

It will give you a preview of the icon. Before tapping Done, make sure and change the name from New Shortcut to whatever you want to call it.

Once you finish, it will show up on your Home screen just like any other app.

Continuity and Handoff

iPadOS 15 includes some incredible features for those of us who work on multiple iPadOS 15 and Sierra and Yosemite OSX devices. Now, when your computer is running Yosemite or higher or your iPadOS 15 iPad is connected to the same Wi-Fi network as your iOS 13 iPhone, you can answer calls or send text messages (both iMessages and regular SMS messages) from your iPad or computer.

The Handoff feature is present in apps like Numbers, Safari, Mail and many more. Handoff allows you to leave an app on one device mid-action and pick up right where you left off on a different device. It makes life much easier for those of us living a multi-gadget lifestyle.

Chapter 6: Using the Camera

Taking Photos and Videos

Now that you know how to make a tablet call, let's get back to the fun stuff! I'll look at using the Photo app next.

The Camera app is on your Home screen, but you can also get to it from your Lock screen for quick, easy access.

The Camera app is pretty simple to use. First, you should know that the Camera app has two cameras; one on the front and one on the back.

The front camera has a lower resolution and is mostly used for self-portraits; it still takes excellent photos, but just remember the back camera is better. To access it, tap the button in the top right corner (the one with the camera and two arrows). The bar on the bottom has all your camera modes. This is how you can switch from photo to video mode.

On the side of the screen you will see a lightning button. That's your flash. Tap this button and you can toggle between different flash modes.

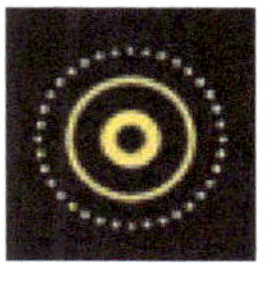

The next two buttons you won't use quite as much. The first, the circle, is for live photos. Live photos takes a short video while you take the photo; it's so quick you won't even know it did it. It's on automatically, so tap it once to turn it off; if you tap and hold a photo with live photo enabled, then you will see the video. Next to that is a timer, which, as you might expect, delays the shot so you can take a group photo.

One of the photo modes is called "Pano" or Panorama. Panorama is the ability to take an extra-long photo that's over 20 megapixels in size. To use it tap the Panorama button. On-screen instructions will now appear. Simply press the Shoot button at the bottom of the screen, and rotate the camera as straight as possible while following the line. When it reaches the end, the photo will automatically go into your album.

The mode you've probably seen the most about is Portrait mode. Portrait mode gives your photos that blurred effect you see on high-end DSLR cameras.

Whether a user is a selfie lover or a photo portrait addict, these are two features all users will appreciate.

To access and use Portrait mode and Portrait Light mode on the iPad mini:

Bring up the Camera app.

Swipe up or down to switch to the Portrait setting.

Line up the shot within 2-8 feet of the subject. The camera's face and body detection will automatically identify the subject and provide instruction to move further or get closer to the subject.

Pay attention to the Camera app's prompts: more light required, flash may help, place subject within 8 feet, or move farther away.

When the shot is ready a banner will appear at the bottom.

Swipe or tap on the cube icons above the shutter button to change lighting effects.

Press the Shutter button to take the photo.

There are several different Portrait modes (Studio Lighting, for example), but you can switch modes after you take the photo; so, if you take it with Studio Lighting, but decide another mode would look better, then you can change it.

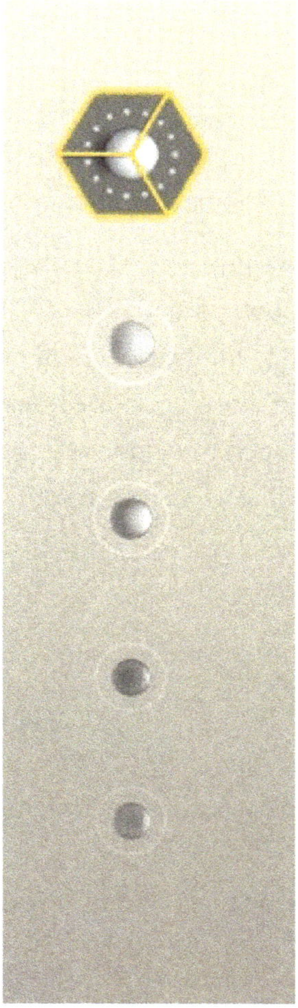

PHOTO EDITING

Editing your photos is just as easy as taking them. As simple as editing tools are, they are also quite powerful. If you want more power though, you can always download one of the hundreds of photo editing apps in the App Store.

To edit a photo, tap the Photo icon on your Home screen.

When you launch Photos, you will see a tab with three buttons; right now, I'll be talking about the Photos button, but we'll talk about Photo Stream in the next chapter. Tap Albums and let's get editing!

Next, tap the photo you want to edit and then tap Edit in the upper-right corner. This will open the editing menu. On the bottom of the screen, you will see all the options: undo, auto correct (which corrects the color of the photo), color change, red eye removal, and finally crop.

The only added feature is the middle one, which lets you change the color saturation.

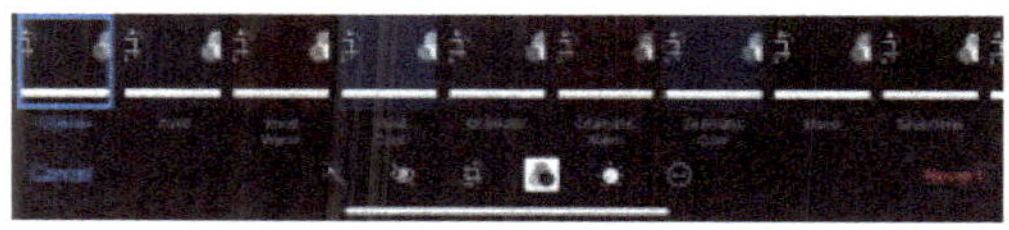

When you are satisfied with the changes tap Save in the upper right corner.

Remember, whenever you want to get to the previous screen just tap the Back button in the upper-left corner.

Live Photos

Apple introduced Live Photos in 2015, when the iPhone 6s came out. This feature enhances the tablets photography, using pictures that move. iPadOS 15 makes Live Photos better than ever. Wanna know how to take a live photo? Let's have a look.

Live Photos records what happens 1.5 seconds before and after you take the photo. That means you're not only getting a photo, you're also getting movement and sound.

Open the Camera app;

Set your camera to Photo mode, and turn Live Photos on;

Hold the tablet very still;

Tap .

With your iPad mini, Live Photos is naturally on by default. If you want to take a still image, tap  and you'll be allowed to turn off Live Photos. If you want Live Photos to always be off, go to Settings > Camera > Preserve Settings.

Photo Albums and Photo Sharing

So now that your photo is taken and edited, let's see how to share photos.

There are several ways to share photos. When you open a photo, you will see an option bar on the bottom. The older version had more options—these options have now been moved to one central place, which you will see next.

The first button lets you share the photo socially and to media devices.

The top row is more of the social options; the bottom row is more of the media options. AirPlay, for example, let's you wirelessly send the photos if you have an Apple TV.

Finally, the last button lets you delete the photo, don't worry about accidently deleting a photo, because it asks you to confirm if you want to delete the photo before you delete it.

Next, let's go to the middle tab. Photo Stream is sort of like Flickr; it lets you share your photos with your family and friends easily. To get to Photo Stream, tap the Shared button on the bottom of the Photo app.

On the top left corner is a '+' button; tap it.

This brings up a menu that lets you create a shared directory. From there you can choose the name, who sees it and if it's a public or private photo stream. To choose a person in your contacts tap the blue '+' button.

Once the album is created, tap the '+' button and tap on each photo you want to add, then hit done.

Once your family or friend accepts your Stream invitation, you will automatically begin syncing your photos. Anytime you add a photo to your album, they will receive a notification.

The new iPadOS will now also group your photos as memories; it does this by looking at where the photo was taken and when it was taken. So, you'll start noticing groups like "Christmas Memories."

Photo Captioning

Swiping up on a photo lets you make changes and add filters, and it also lets you add a caption; captions can later be searched. So you can add something like "Grand Canyon Vacation" and later search for that term.

Hide Photos

We all have embarrassing photos—you know, the ones with you dressed in a tutu while riding a unicorn? Or is that just me?!

If you want to hide "certain" photos so only you can see them, then that's an option. It used to be you could hide them, but they would show up in your albums. They were "kind of" hidden, but I think most people would agree that they weren't so much hidden as harder to find.

In iPadOS 15, the ability was added to completely hide that folder. Go to the Settings app, and then Photos; scroll to Hidden Album. If it's toggled on, the Hidden Album will be in the Utilities area of albums (like I said, harder to find, but not really hidden); if it's toggled off, it's gone. Like nowhere to be found. The images are saved and stored in the cloud —even though you can't see them. To see them, toggle it back on, then go to Albums and scroll to Utilities. If you know a celebrity, then pass this information on to them, so we can stop hearing about all those "accidental" shares of photos meant to be private.

To hide a photo, find it, then select it and tap the Share icon; this brings up how you want to share it (kind of a misleading name, isn't it—you're hiding it because you don't want to share it!); one of the options is Hide—tap that.

It will confirm that you actually want to hide it. If you change your mind later, then you go into the hidden album and unhide it the same way. You can also select several images at a time to hide them as a group.

Lift Photo out of Background

Pictures in texts and documents are fun. You know what's better? Remove the background so the image really stands out!

Open up a photo, then tap the portion you want to pull out from the background. Next, select copy.

Next, go to the application you want to paste it into. I'm using the Notes app, but you can use a text message, email, or lots of other apps. From here, you'll tap and hold, then select paste.

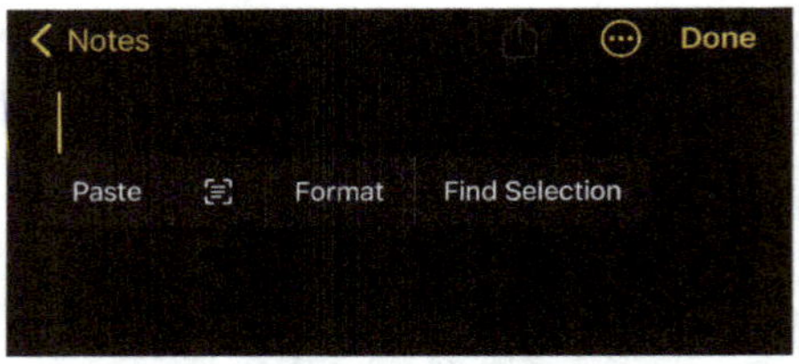

Look at that! A photo is pasted with the background removed!

Lookup

Imagine: you just saw the most adorable dog. You want to know what breed it is. Photos has an easy solution: take a picture and then look it up. Take a look at the puppy below. Adorable, right? But what exactly is it? When you swipe up over a photo of a dog, you can see.

After swiping up, assuming it recognizes it's a dog, it will have a paw print icon. Tap on that.

It will now bring back what it calls "Siri Knowledge" which is articles about the breed it thinks it is. It will also show similar photos. Is it always right? It's a computer, so no—that's especially true with mutts that have several breeds.

This feature isn't limited to dogs. You can use it with other animals and even landmarks. In the photo below, it thinks it knows where this image was taken and it will show it on a map—if it was a landmark, it would also provide articles about the image.

Live Text

In addition to articles about an animal or place in a photo, you can also copy text out of a photo. You just have to make sure the text is sharp enough. This is especially helpful for things like phone numbers. Want to call a business? Just take a picture of the sign with the number, then tap the number in the image and you can call from the photo.

Shared Library

Sharing an album is nothing new in iOS. Sharing a library is something quite different, however. Sharing a library gives people access to all of your photos—or photos that you give them permission to see—a date range, for example. One of the cool features to this is you can share directly to that folder when you take a picture. Let's take a look at how to set it up and how it works.

To get started, you have to go into your Settings. From Settings, navigate to Photos, then click the Shared Library option.

This brings you into a very simple set of instructions for setting things up; just tap the blue Get Started option to get started.

Next, you'll add the contacts you want to

add to sharing—be careful here: since it's sharing all of your photos, you probably will only want to select immediate family.

Next, select what you want to share: all of your photos, a date range of photos, or manually choose.

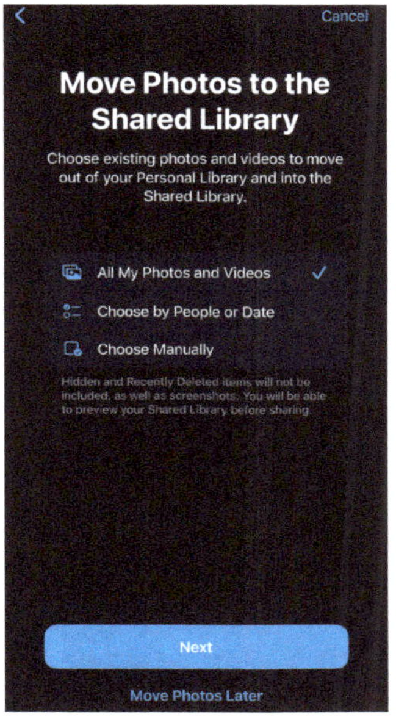

Next, it will give you a preview of what you are sharing. If you have been an iPhone user for a while, it might be quite large—you can see in my case that I am sharing nearly 50,000 photos, and 4,000 videos. If you are sharing something similar, you'll probably see a processing screen for an extended amount of time.

From here, you'll decide how you are inviting them to see the photos.

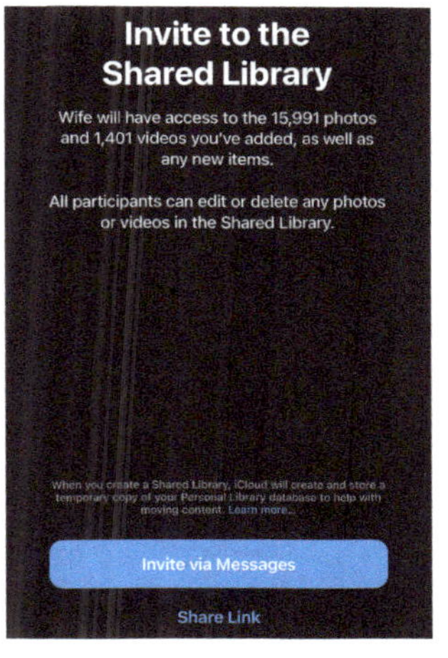

It will just put a small thumbnail with the link in the message that you send.

It will also ask you if you want to share directly from the camera—that means it shares what you take a photo of.

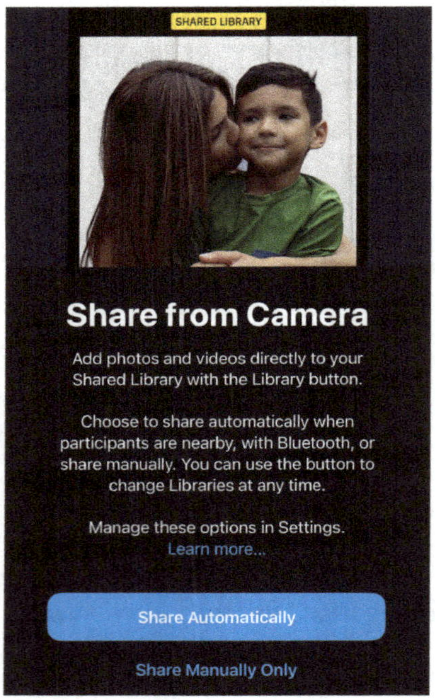

Once you answer the question about the camera, you are ready to start sharing.

You'll now notice when you go into photos that when you click the little three dots in the upper right corner of all photos, there's an option to view your different libraries.

Head into your camera app, and you'll also see a little person icon either toggled on or off.

Off means you aren't sharing the photos that you take pictures of in your Shared Library; toggled on means that you are.

Chapter 7: Hey, Siri

By now, you probably know all about Siri and how it can remind you of things. If not, say, "Hey, Siri."

Siri works the same as always, but she's gotten a few under-the-hood updates to make her faster.

The biggest change to Siri is the look. The theme of many of the changes to iOS is how do you minimize what already works. With Siri that means having a smaller look. It now launches in a more nonintrusive way.

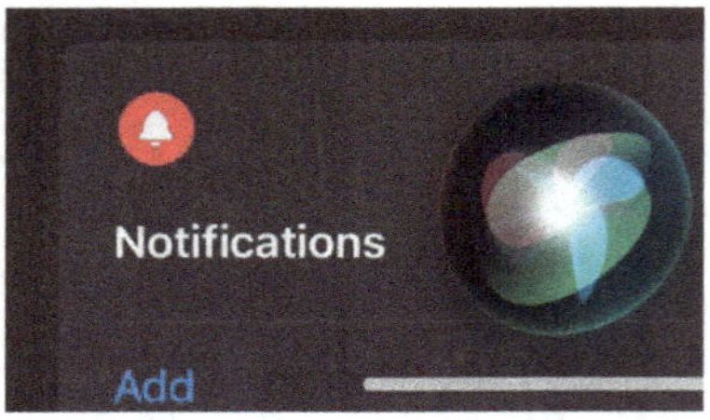

Her replies also go with fewer distractions. She used to launch full-screen replies that took you out of what you were doing to see the answer. Now it just takes a little bit of space.

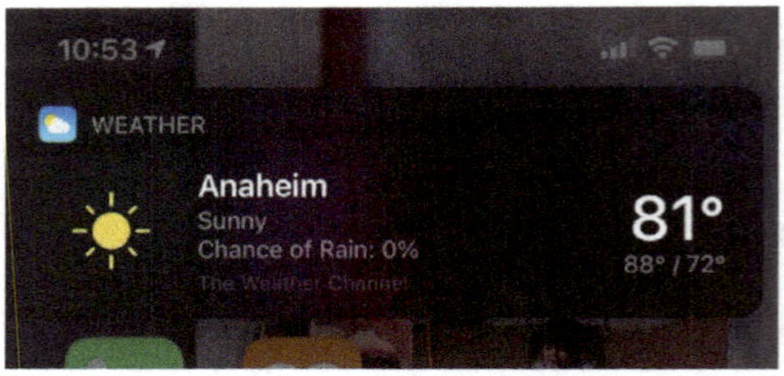

So, what exactly do you do with it? The first thing you should do is introduce Siri to your family. Siri is pretty smart, and she wants to meet your family. To introduce her to your family, activate Siri and say: "Brian is my brother" or "Susan is my boss." Once you confirm the relationship you can now say things like: "Call my brother" or "email my boss."

Siri is also location-based. What does that mean? It means that instead of saying: "Remind me to call wife at 8 am" you can say: "Remind me when I leave work to call wife" and as soon as you step out of the office you will receive a reminder. Siri can be a bit frustrating at first, but it's one of the tablet's most powerful apps, so give it a chance!

Everyone hates dealing with waits. There's nothing worse than being hungry and having to wait an hour for a table. Siri does her best to make your life easier by making reservations for you. For this to work, you'll need a free app called OpenTable (you'll also need a free account), which is in the Apple App Store. This app makes its money by restaurants paying it, so don't worry about having to pay to use it. Once it's installed, you will simply activate Siri and say: "Hey Siri, make me a reservation at the Olive Garden," (or wherever you want to eat). Note that not all restaurants participate in OpenTable, but hundreds (if not thousands) do, and it's growing monthly, so if it's not there it probably will be soon.

Siri is ever evolving. And with the latest update, Apple has taught her everything she needs to know about sports. Go ahead, try it! Say something like: "Hey, Siri. What's the score in the Kings game?" or: "Who leads the league in homeruns?"

Siri has also got a little wiser in movies. You can say: "Movies directed by Peter Jackson" and it will give you a list and let you see a synopsis, the review rating from Rotten Tomatoes, and in some cases even a trailer or an option to buy the movie. You can also say: "Movie show times" and a list of nearby movies playing will appear. At this time, you cannot buy tickets to the movie, though one can imagine that option will be coming very soon.

Finally, Siri can open apps for you. If you want to open an app, simply say: "Open and the apps name."

The new iPadOS lets you add shortcuts to Siri; you can see this in Settings > Siri & Search > Shortcuts.

CHAPTER 8: APPLE SERVICES

INTRODUCTION

It used to be a few times a year Apple would take the stage and announce something that everyone's head exploded over! The iPhone! The iPad! The Apple Watch! The iPod!

That still happens today, but Apple also is well aware of the reality: most people don't upgrade to new hardware every year. How does a company make money when that happens? In a word: services.

In the past few years (especially in 2019) Apple announced several services—things people would opt into to pay for monthly. It was a way to continue making money even when people were not buying hardware.

For it to work, Apple knew they couldn't just offer a subpar service and expect people to pay because it said Apple. It had to be good. And it is!

This book will walk you through some of those services and show you how to get the most out of them.

ICLOUD

iCloud is something that Apple doesn't talk a lot about but is perhaps their biggest service. It's estimated that nearly

850 million people use it. The thing about it, however, is many people don't even know they're using it.

What exactly is it? If you are familiar with Google Drive, then the concept is something you probably already understand. It's an online storage locker. But it's more than that. It is a place where you can store files, and it also syncs everything—so if you send a message on your iPhone, it appears on your MacBook and iPad. If you work on a Keynote presentation from your iPad, you can continue where you left off on your iPhone.

What's even better about iCloud is it's affordable. New phones get 5GB for free. From there the price range is as follows (note that these prices may change after printing):

- 50GB: $0.99
- 200GB: $2.99
- 2TB: $9.99

These prices are for everyone in your family. So, if you have five people on your plan, then each person doesn't need their own storage plan. This also means purchases are saved—if one family member buys a book or movie, everyone can access it.

iCloud has become even more powerful as our photo library grows. Photos used to be relatively small, but as cameras have advanced, the size goes up. Most photos on your phone are several MB big. iCloud means you can keep the newest ones on your phone and put the older ones in the Cloud. It also means you don't have to worry about paying for the phone with the biggest hard drive—in fact, even if you have the biggest hard drive, there's a chance it won't fit all of your photos.

Where Is iCloud?

If you look at your iPad, you won't see an iCloud app. That's because there isn't an iCloud app. There's a Files app that functions like a storage locker.

To see iCloud, point your computer browser to iCloud.com.

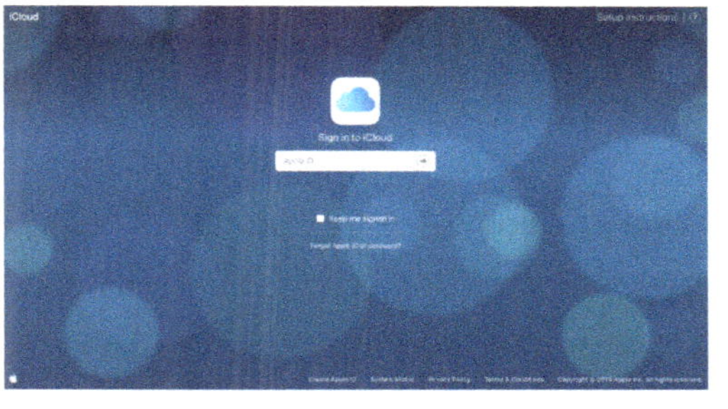

Once you sign in, you'll see all the things stored in your Cloud—photos, contacts, notes, files; these are all things you can access across all of your devices.

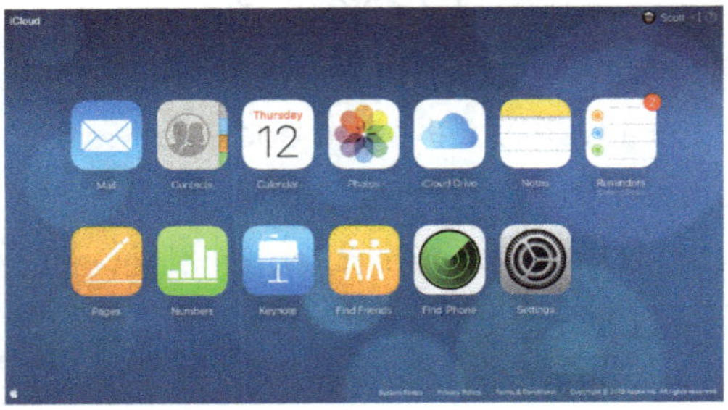

In addition, you can use iCloud from any computer (even PCs); this is especially helpful if you need to use Find My, which locates not only your iPhone, but all of your Apple devices—phones, watches, even AirPods.

Backing Up Your Phone With iCloud

The first thing you should know about iCloud is how to back up your phone with it. This is what you will need to do if you are moving from one phone to another.

If there's no iCloud app on the phone, then how do you do that? While there is no native app in the traditional sense that you are used to, there are several iCloud settings in the Settings app.

Open the Settings app; at the top you will see your name and profile picture; tap that.

This opens my ID settings where I can update things like phone numbers and email. One of the options is iCloud. Tap that.

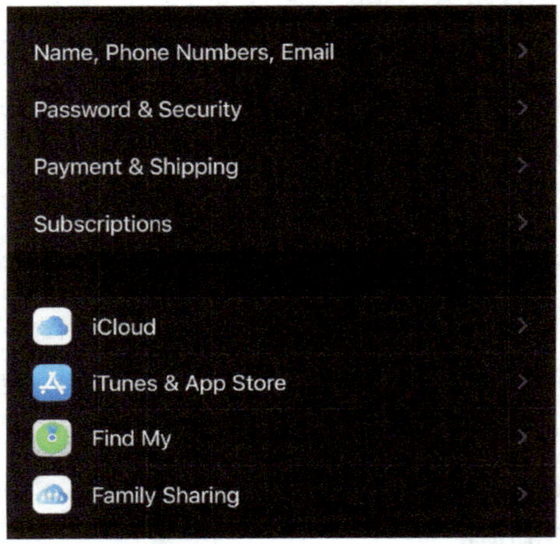

Scroll down a little until you get to the setting that says iCloud Backup, and tap that.

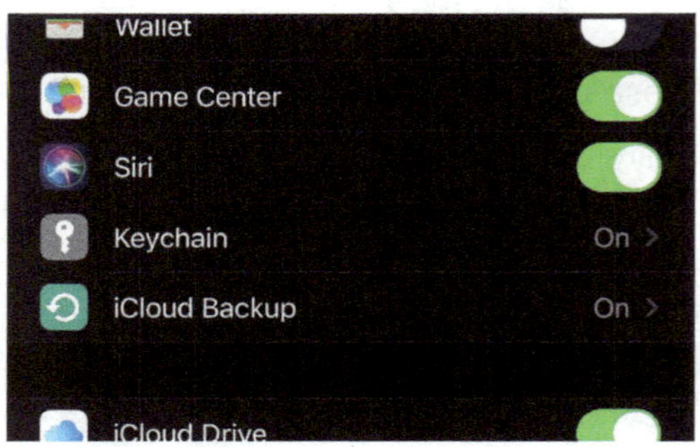

It will probably be on (the toggle switch will be green); if you'd rather do things manually, then you can toggle it off and then do Back Up Now. If you turn it off, then you'll have to do a manual backup each time.

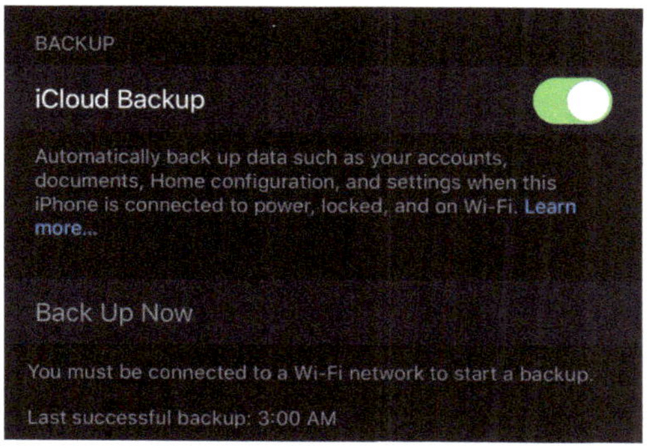

From the iCloud, you'll also be able to change what apps use iCloud and see how much space you have left. In my case, I have the 2TB plan, and we've used about half of it.

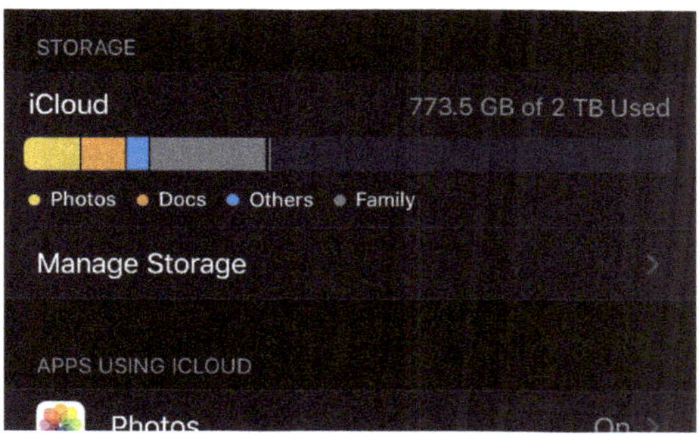

If you tap Manage Storage, you can see where the storage is being used. You can also upgrade or downgrade your account from this page by tapping on Change Storage Plan.

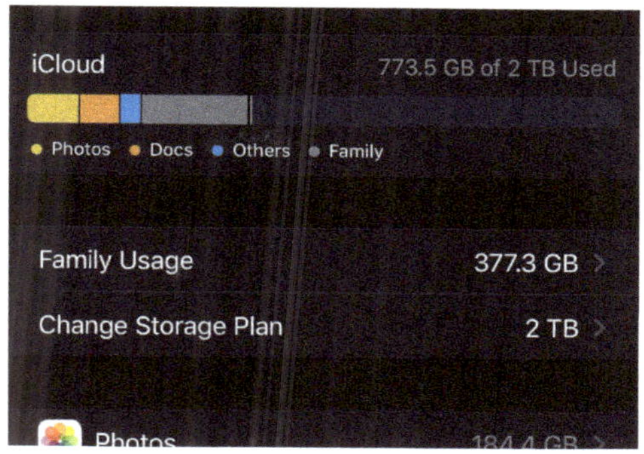

Tap on Family Usage and you can see more specifically which family members use what. You can also stop sharing from this page.

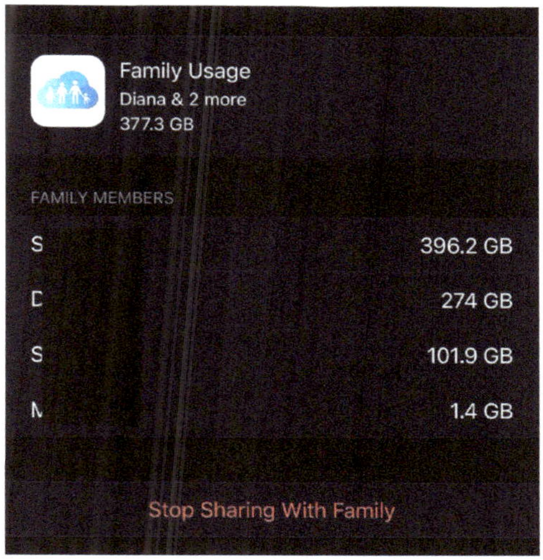

Moving to a New Device

When you get a new device, you will be asked during the setup to log in with your Apple ID associated with your previous device, and then get the option to recover from a previous device.

Sharing Photos With iCloud

To share and backup photos with iCloud, go into Settings > Photos and ensure iCloud Photos is toggled to green. If you are short on storage, you can check the option below to Optimize Storage.

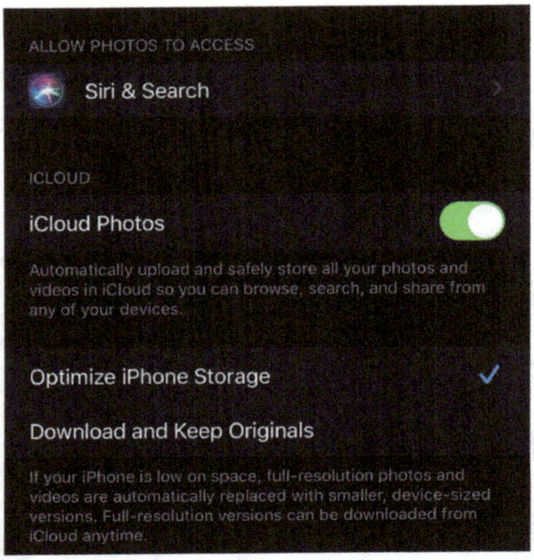

Files App

To see your cloud files, open the Files app.

The first thing you'll see is all your recent files.

If you don't see what you are looking for, then go to the bottom tabs and switch from Recents to Browse.

This opens a more traditional looking file explorer.

If you want to create a new folder, connect to a server, or scan a document, tap and hold anywhere on your screen.

Scan Documents lets you use your camera like a traditional flatbed scanner to scan and print documents.

You can also access this option by tapping on locations, then tapping on the three small dots.

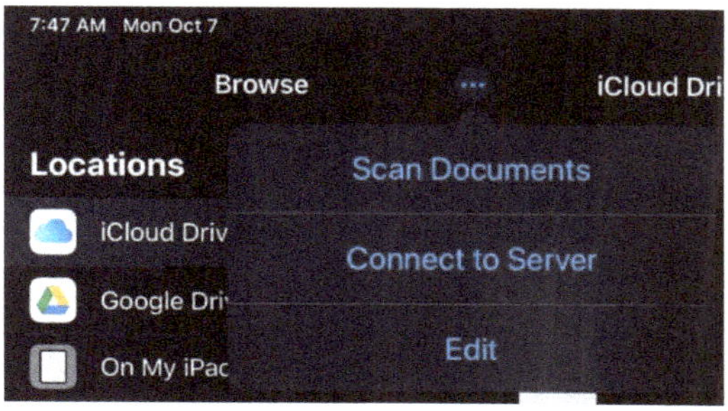

You can drag up from the top to reveal a hidden sort menu (where you can also create a new folder).

Tapping and holding on any of the icons will reveal a menu option that lets you share, rename, and more to a file.

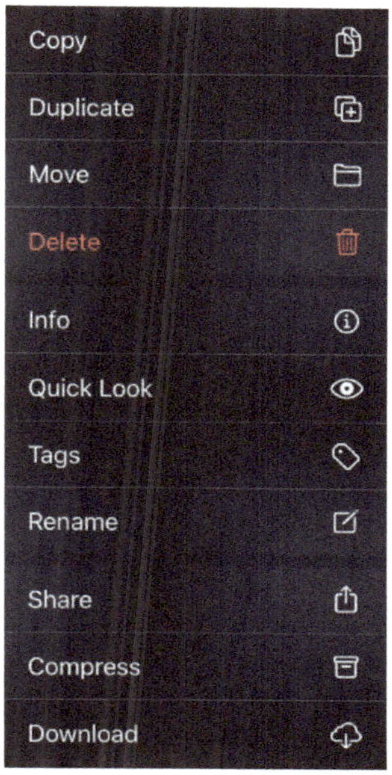

iCloud Settings

One other important set of iCloud settings is in Settings > General > iPad Storage.

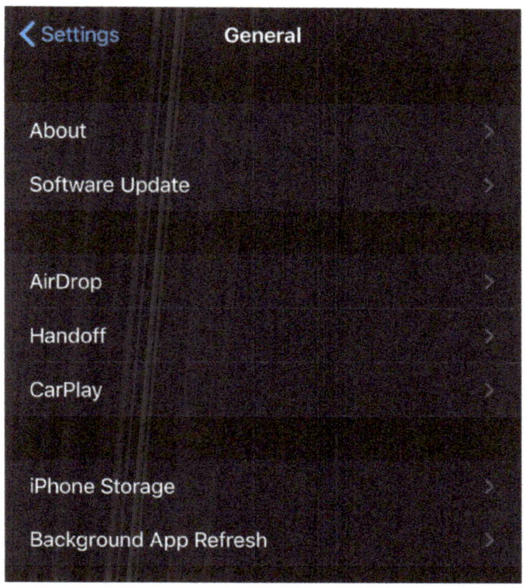

When you tap this, it will show you how much storage apps are using and also make recommendations.

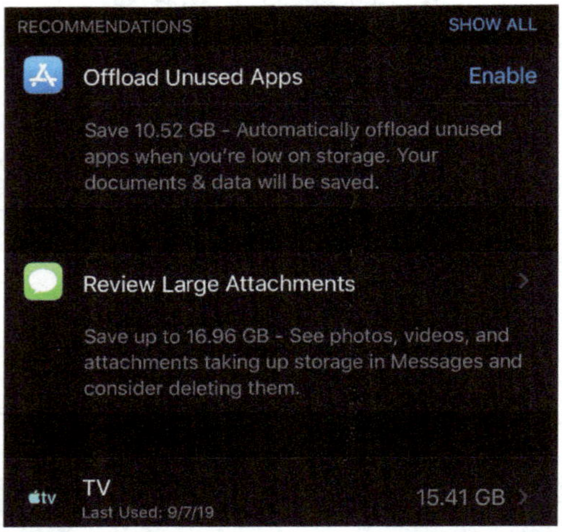

Apple Music

Apple Music is Apple's music streaming service.

The question most people wonder is which is better: Spotify or Apple Music? On paper it's hard to tell. They both have the same number of songs, and they both cost the same ($9.99 a month, $5 for students, $14.99 for families).

There really is no clear winner. It all comes down to preference. Spotify has some good features—such as an ad-supported free plan.

One of the standout features of Apple Music is iTunes Match. If you are like me and have a large collection of audio files on your computer, then you'll love iTunes Match. Apple puts those files in the Cloud, and you can stream them on any of your devices. This feature is also available if you don't have Apple Music for $25 a year.

Apple Music also plays well with Apple devices; so, if you are an Apple house (i.e. everything you own, from smart speakers to TV media boxes, has the Apple logo), then Apple Music is probably the best one for you.

Apple is compatible with other smart speakers, but it's built to shine on its own devices.

I won't cover Spotify here, but my advice is to try them both (they both have free trials) and see which interface you prefer.

Apple Music Crash Course

Before going over where things are in Apple Music, it's worth noting that Apple Music can now be accessed from your web browser (in beta form) here: http://beta.music.apple.com.

It's also worth noting that I have a little girl and don't get to listen to a lot of "adult" music, so the examples here are going to show a lot of kids music!

The main navigation on Apple Music is at the bottom. There are five basic menus to select from:

- Library
- For You
- Browse
- Radio
- Search

At the far right is a bar with what's currently playing (if applicable).

LIBRARY

When you create playlists or download songs or albums, this is where you will go to find them.

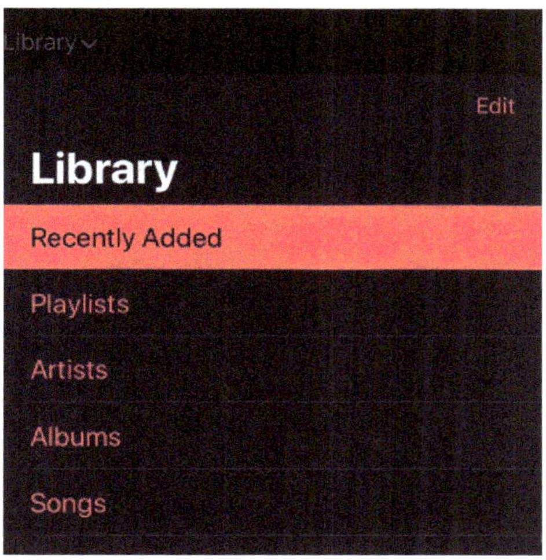

You can change the categories that show up in this first list by tapping on Edit, then checking off the categories you want. Make sure to hit Done to save your changes.

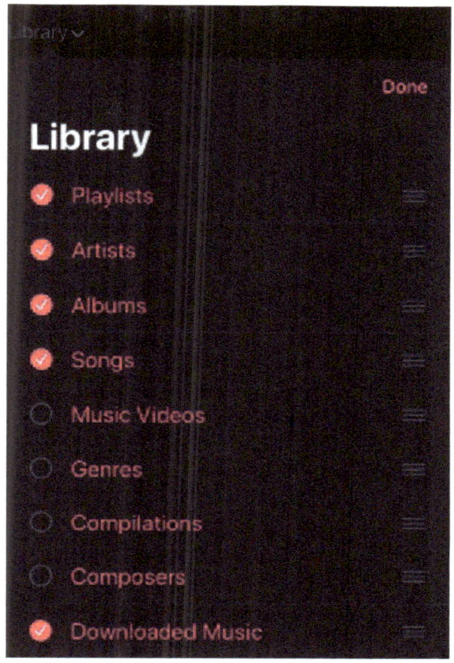

FOR YOU

As you play music, Apple Music starts to get to know you more and more; it makes recommendations based on what you are playing.

In For You, you can get a mix of all these songs and see other recommendations.

In addition to different styles of music, it also has friends' recommendations so you can discover new music based on what your friends are listening to.

Browse

Not digging those recommendations? You can also browse genres in the Browse menu. In addition to different genre categories, you can see what music is new and what music is popular.

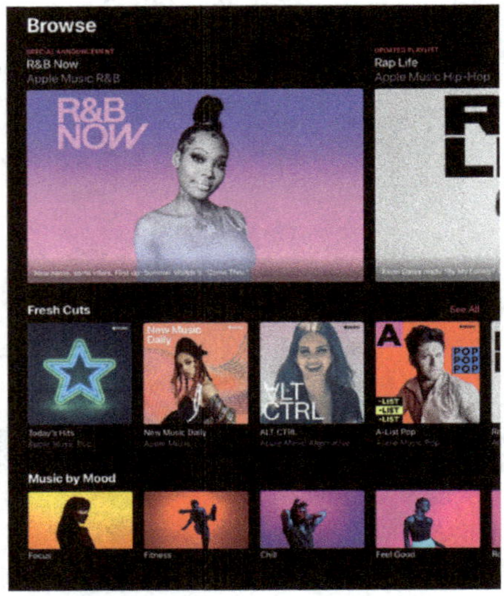

Radio

Radio is Apple's version of AM/FM; the main radio station is Beats One. There are on-air DJs and everything you'd expect from a radio station.

While Beats One is Apple's flagship station, it's not its only station. You can scroll down and tap on Radio Stations under More to explore and see several other stations based on music styles (i.e. country, alternative, rock, etc.). Under this menu, you'll also find a handful of talk stations covering news and sports. Don't expect to find the opinionated talk radio you may listen to on regular radio—it's pretty controversy-free.

Search

The last option is the search menu, which is pretty self-explanatory. Type in what you want to find (i.e. artist, album, genre, etc.).

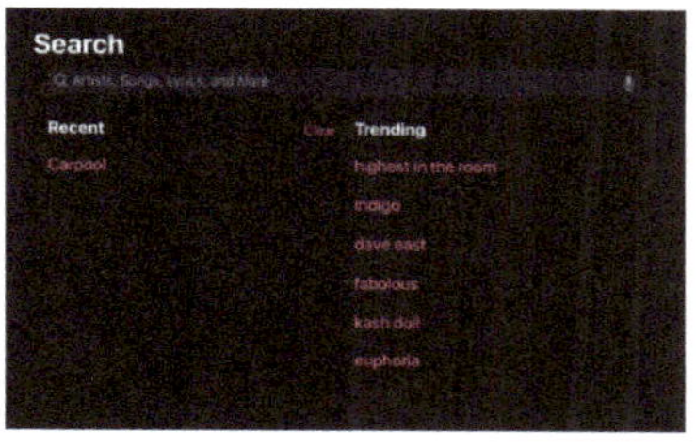

Listening to Music and Creating a Playlist

You can access the music you are currently listening to from the bottom of your screen.

Tapping on this brings up a larger view of what you are listening to with several options.

The play, back/forward, and volume buttons are pretty straightforward. The buttons below that might look new.

The first option is for lyrics. If the song is paused, then you can read through the lyrics; if the song is playing, then it will bold the lyrics to the song it is currently playing. If you ever caught yourself wondering if the singer is saying "dense" or "dance" then this feature is a game changer.

The middle option lets you pick where you play the music. For example, if you have a HomePod and you want to listen wirelessly to the music from that device, you can change it here.

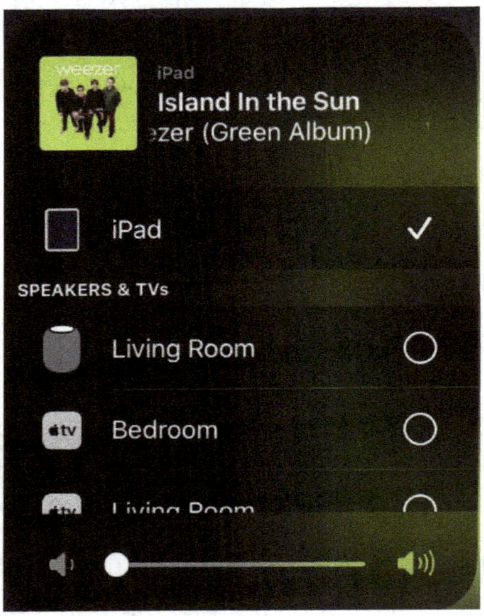

The last option shows the next song(s) in the playlist.

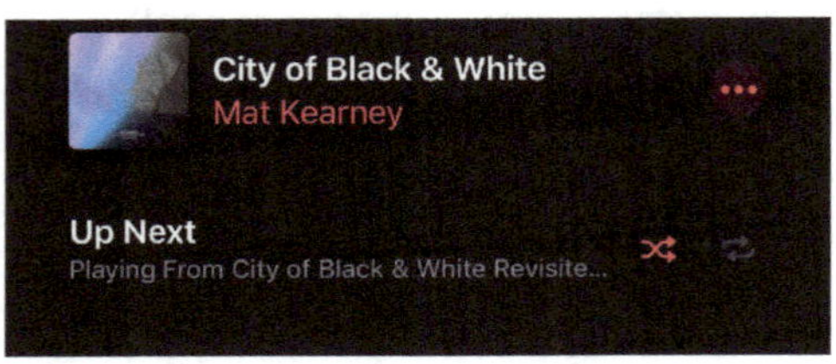

If you want to add a song to a playlist, then click the three dots next to the album/artist name. This brings up a list of several options (you can also go here to love or hate a song—which helps Apple Music figure out what you like); the option you want is Add to a Playlist. If you don't have a playlist or want to add it to a new one, then you can also create one here.

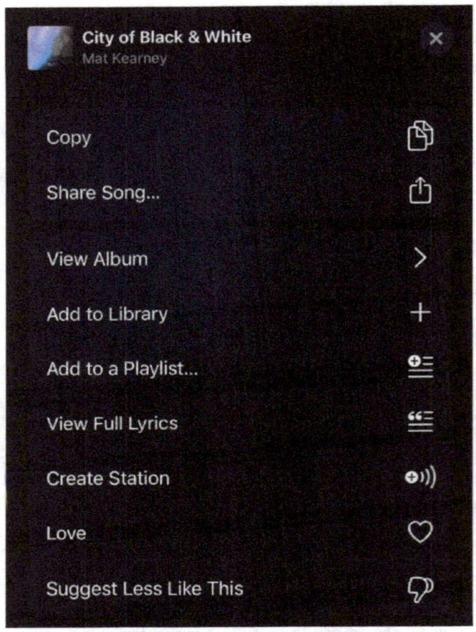

At any point, you can tap the artist's name to see all of their music.

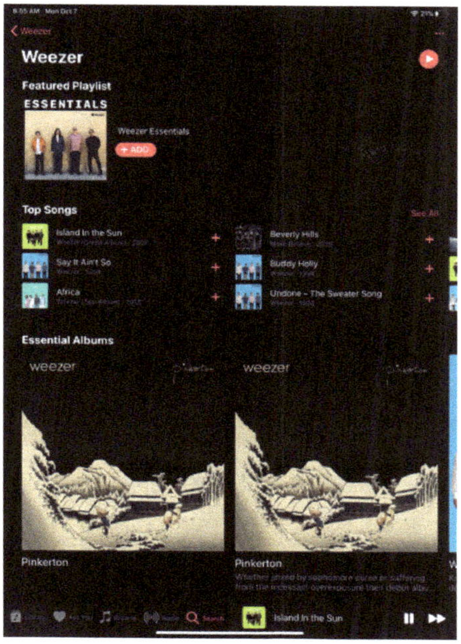

In addition to seeing information about the band, their popular songs, and their albums, you can get a playlist of their essential songs or a playlist of bands that they have influenced.

If you scroll to the bottom, you can also see Similar Artists, which is a great way to discover new bands that are like the ones you are currently listening to.

Tips for Getting the Most Out of Apple Music

Heart It

Like what you're hearing? Heart it! Hate it? Dislike it. Apple gets to know you by what you listen to, but it improves the accuracy when you tell it what you think of a song you are really into…or really hate.

Use Settings

Some of the most resourceful features of Apple Music aren't in Apple Music—they're in your settings.

Open the Settings app and scroll down to Music.

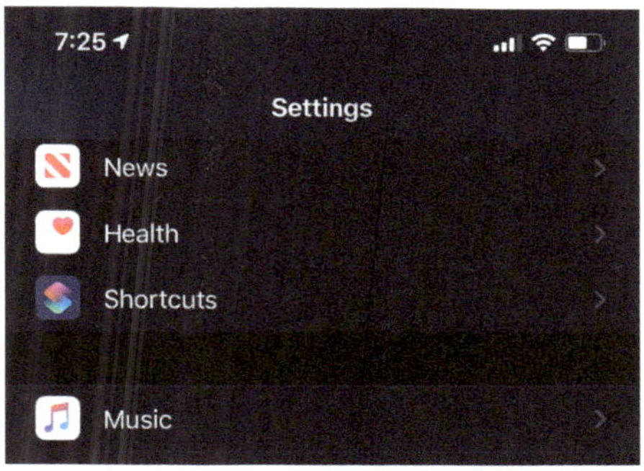

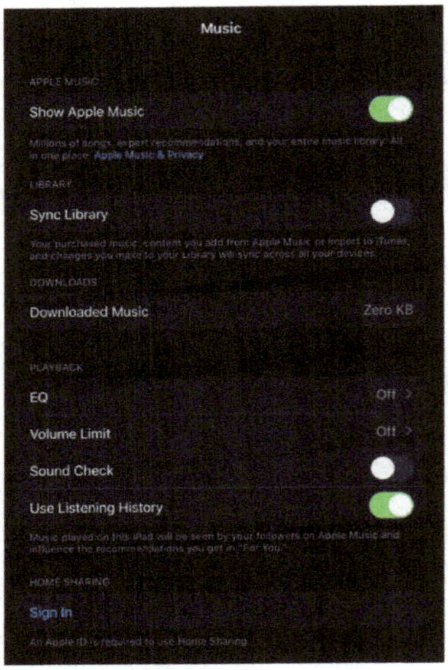

Want to change the way your music sounds—such as more or less bass—go to EQ in the settings.

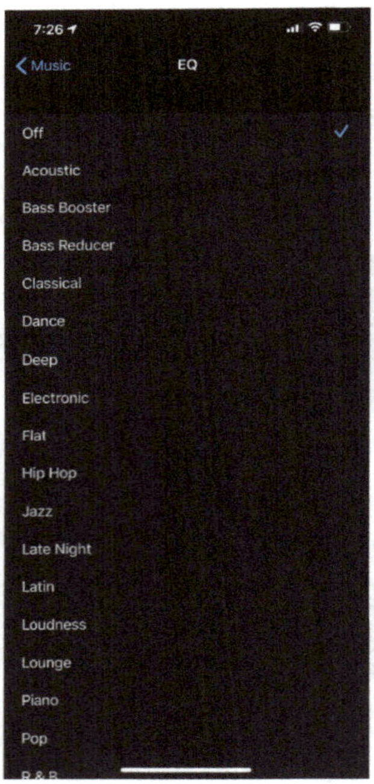

Download Music

If you don't want to rely on data when you are on the go, make sure and tap the cloud on your music to download the music locally to your phone. If you don't see a cloud, add it to your library by tapping the plus, which should change it to a cloud.

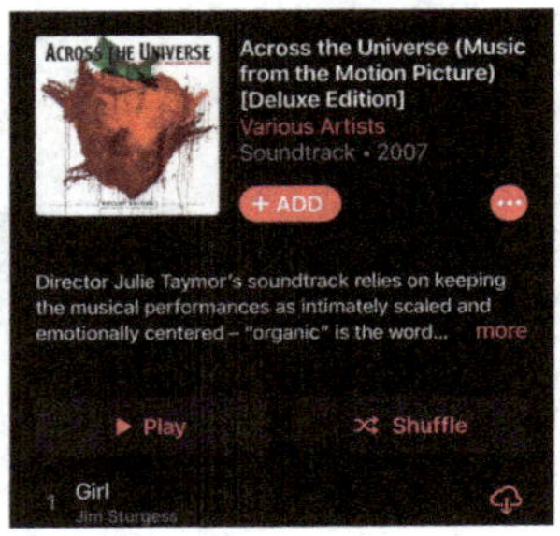

Hey Siri

Siri knows music! Say "Hey Siri," and say what you want to listen to, and the AI will get to work.

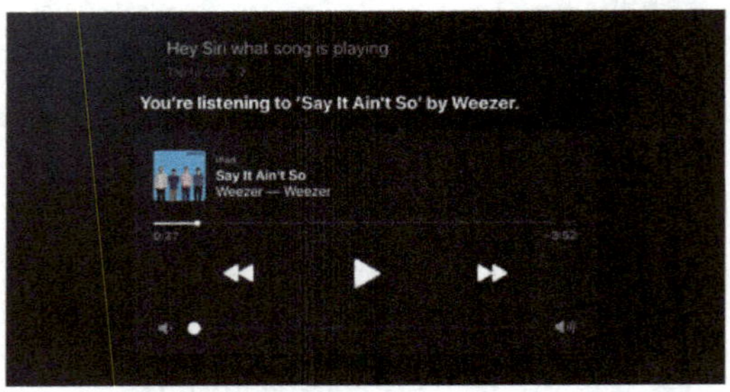

Apple News

In 2012, a little app with big ambitions called Next (it was later changed to Texture) disrupted the magazine industry by creating the Netflix of magazines. For one low price, you could read hundreds of magazines (and their back issues, too). They weren't small indie magazines—they were the big ones: People, Time, Wired, and more.

Apple took notice, and, in 2018, they acquired the company. The writing was on the wall: Apple wanted to get into print services.

In 2019, it was announced that Texture would close because Apple would release a new service called News+. News+ does everything that Texture did, but also combines newspapers (Los Angeles Times and The Wall Street Journal).

There is a free version of the service that curates news for you; the paid version that carries the magazine subscriptions is $9.99. (You can have five family members on your plan.)

What really makes Apple News stand out is it's curated for you and your tastes. If you have other family members on your plan, it will be curated for them as well—it's based on the user's tastes, so if you have a family member into entertainment news and you are into game news, you won't see their interests—only yours.

Apple News Crash Course

To get started, open the News app from your iPad (if it is not on your iPad, it's a free download from the App Store).

The UI for the app is pretty simple. There are several menu options found by swiping from the left of the screen to the right; the two you will use the most:

Today—This is where you'll find your curated news

News+—Where you'll find magazines

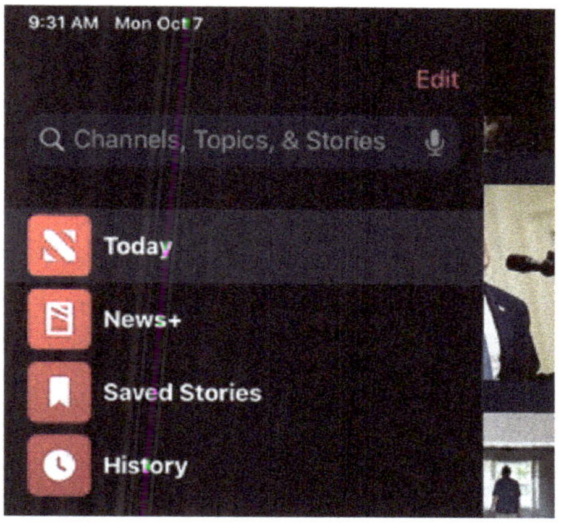

Today

The Today menu gives you all your news (starting with the top news/breaking news) in a scrolling format.

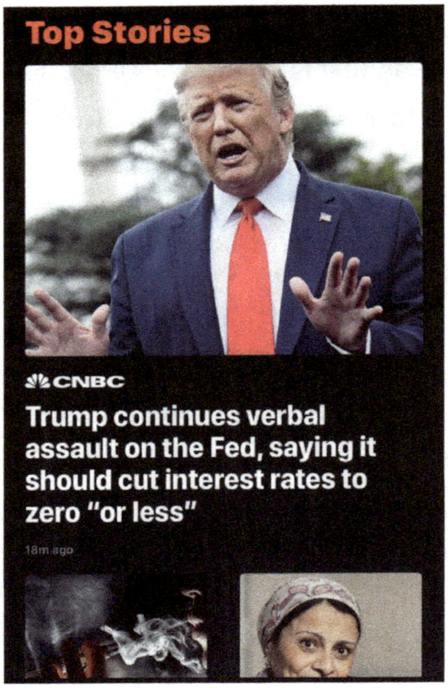

The app relies a lot on gestures. Tap and hold over a story and you'll get several options.

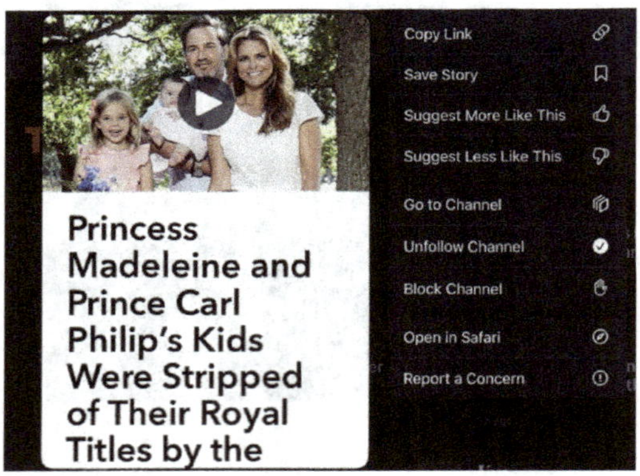

The one you will probably use the most is to suggest more / less like this; these two options help Apple News understand what you are into and will over time start to personalize stories based on your preferences.

Typically, "report" in a news app means you find it somehow inappropriate in nature; that's true here, but there are other reasons to report it—such as, it's dated wrong, it's in the wrong category, it's a broken link, or something else.

As you scroll down, you start seeing different categories (Trending Stories in the example below); when you tap the three dots with a circle, you'll get an option to block it, so it won't show in your feed any longer.

When you tap to read a story, there are only a few options. At the top, there's the option to make the text larger or smaller; next to that is the option to share the story with friends (assuming they have Apple News). To get to the next story, there's an option in the lower right corner (or swipe left from the right corner of the screen); to get back to the previous page, tap the back arrow in the upper left corner or swipe right from the left side of the screen.

One criticism of Apple News by some has been its UI; when Apple announced the service along with its partnership with the Los Angeles Times and Wall Street Journal, many expected a format similar to what you have seen with the magazines section—a full newspaper-type layout.

Worse, many didn't even know how to find the newspaper. And if they did find it, they couldn't search for stories. While the app is pretty resourceful, this is still an early product and some of the features you want might not be there yet.

That said, you can "kind of" read the Los Angeles Times (or any newspaper in Apple News) in a more traditional way. First, find an article in your feed from the publication you want to see more from, and then click the publication's name at the top of the story.

Los Angeles Times

This will bring up the publication along with all the topics from that publication.

If you want to search for a particular story or publication, then swipe from the left of the screen to the right, and search for what you want to find.

Following

At any time, you can swipe from the left edge of the screen to the right and see the channels / topics that you follow.

This is where you are going to be able to look at your history, read saved stories (as noted above), search for stories and publications, and follow or unfollow topics.

To unfollow a category, swipe left over it and select unfollow.

To add a new category, scroll down a little. You'll see suggested topics. Tap the '+' button for any you want to follow.

You can move your categories around by tapping on the Edit button at the top right.

News+

The last section to cover is News+; this is where you'll find all the magazines you love.

The format is similar to the Today screen; magazines you read are at the top; below that are stories pulled from several different magazines that the app thinks you'll be interested in. There's also a more personalized For You section.

When you read articles from the list, it opens in the actual magazine and looks a little different from articles in the Today area.

Anytime you want to read more from a magazine (or see back issues) just click the logo from an article you are reading.

That brings up a list of all the issues you can read as well as some of the latest stories from the magazine.

Tapping the '+' button in the upper right corner will let you follow the publication.

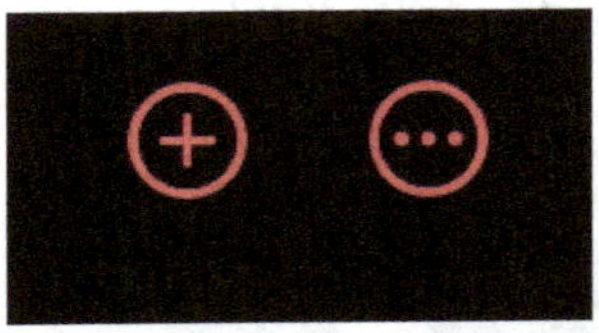

If you long press (press and hold) the magazine cover from your My Magazines section, you can also unfollow, delete, or see back issues from the publication.

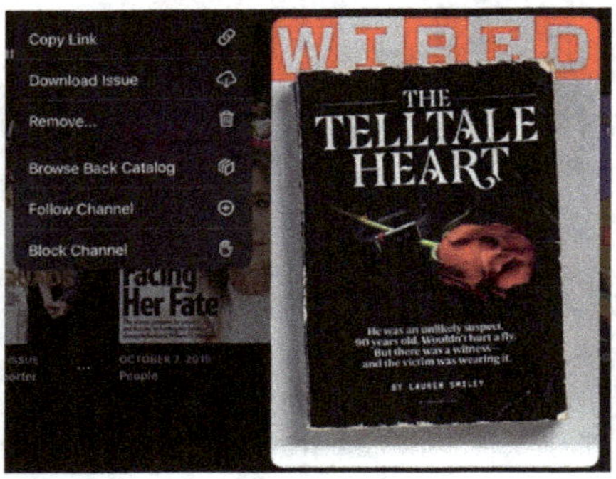

To browse all the magazines available, select Browse the Catalog from the main screen (or browse by a category that you are interested in).

This brings up a list of all the magazines you can read (at this writing, there are around 300).

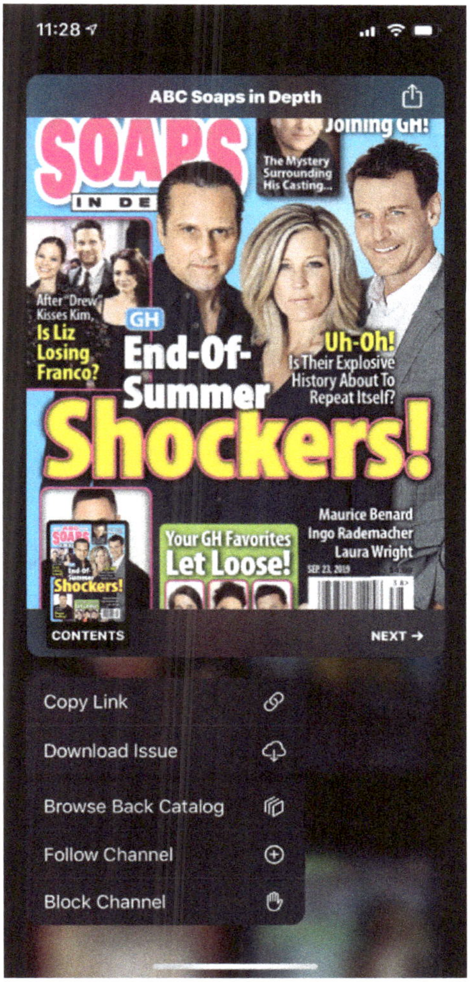

Long press any of them and you can download the magazine, follow it, block it, or browse the back-issue library.

Fitness+

One of the biggest improvements coming to Apple Devices is Fitness+. This is going to be a new Apple Service that is set to disrupt the fitness industry.

It will costs $9.99 a month or $79.99 a year (with three months free if you buy a new Apple Watch); Fitness+ will also be bundled into the new Apple One Premier service ($29.99 / month), which gives you and your entire family access to all Apple Services.

The way the services will work is you pick the type of workout you want to do using either your Apple TV, iPad, or iPhone; this will sync up instantly with your watch. So while the video workout is playing, you'll see things like your heart rate on the video.

The workouts will change every week, and you can use them with or without exercise equipment. There are workouts for beginners and advance users, and Apple's AI will recommend different workouts and trainers based on your workout regiment.

You can even filter the workouts by time (from 5 minutes to 45 minutes); so if you only have a few minutes in your schedule, you can find a workout routine that fits into that schedule.

If you have used (or are familiar with) Peloton, then its a very similar concept. The biggest difference is it can work with more devices (or no device at all); that makes it great for traveling.

You'll also be able to choose the type of music that plays during your workout.

Chapter 9: Maintenance

Security

Passcode (dos and don'ts, tips, etc.)

In this day and age, it's important to keep your device secure. You may or may not want to set up a Touch ID (if it's on your model), but at the very least it's a good idea to maintain a passcode. Anytime your tablet is unlocked, restarted, updated, or erased, it will require a passcode before allowing entry into the tablet. To set up a passcode for your iPad, go to Settings > Passcode, and click on Turn Passcode On. You will be prompted to enter a 4-digit or 6-digit passcode, then re-enter to confirm. Here are a few tips to follow for maximum security:

Encryption

With all of the personal and sensitive information that can be stored on iCloud, security is understandably a very real concern. Apple agrees with this, and protects your data with high level 128-bit AES encryption. Keychain, which you will learn about next, uses 256-bit AES encryption—the same level of encryption used by all of the top banks who need high levels of security for their data. According to Apple, the only things not protected with encryption through iCloud is Mail (because email clients already provide their own security) and iTunes in the Cloud, since music does not contain any personal information.

Keychain

Have you logged onto a website for the first time in ages and forgotten what kind of password you used? This happens to everyone; some websites require special characters or phrases, while others require small 8-character passwords. iCloud comes with a highly encrypted feature called Keychain that allows you to store passwords and login information in one place. Any of your Apple devices synced with the same iCloud account will be able to load the data from Keychain without any additional steps.

To activate and start using Keychain, simply click on Settings > iCloud and toggle Keychain on, then follow the prompts. After you've added accounts and passwords to Keychain, your Safari browser will automatically fill in fields while you remain logged into iCloud. If you are ready to checkout after doing some online shopping, for example, the credit card information will automatically pre-fill, so you don't have to enter any sensitive information at all.

iCloud

To really get the full effect of Apple's carefully created ecosystem and be a part of it, you will need to create an iCloud account. Simply put, iCloud is a powerful cloud system that will seamlessly coordinate all of your important devices. The Cloud can be a little difficult to understand, but the best way to think about it is like a storage unit that lives in a secure part of the internet. You are allocated a certain amount of space, and you can put the things that mean the most to you here to keep safe. In the case of iCloud, Apple gives you 5 GB for free.

Your tablet lets you automatically back up certain files such as your photos, mail, contacts, calendars, reminders, and notes. In the event that your tablet is damaged beyond repair or is lost or stolen, your data will still be stored safely on iCloud. To retrieve your information, you can either log onto iCloud.com on a Mac or PC, or log into your iCloud account on another iPad to load the information onto that tablet.

With the introduction of iOS 8 and the iPhone 6 and 6 Plus, Apple rolled out a few major changes. You will now be able to store even more types of documents using iCloud Drive and access them from any smartphone, tablet, or computer. Additionally, up to six family members will now be able to share purchases from iTunes, and the App Store, removing the need to buy an app twice simply because you and a loved one have two different iCloud accounts.

For users who will need more than 5 GB, Apple has dramatically reduced the cost of iCloud:

50 GB is $0.99 per month

200 GB is $2.99 per month

1 TB (1000 GB) is $9.99 per month

2 TB (2000 GB) is $19.99 per month

Battery Tips

The iPad promises amazing battery life. But let's face it, no matter how great the battery is, you probably would love to have just a little bit more life in your charge.

Disable Notifications

My mom told me her battery didn't seem to be lasting very long. I looked at her tablet and could not believe how many notifications were activated. She knows absolutely nothing about stocks, nor does she have any desire to learn, and yet she had stock tickers going. You might want notifications on something like Facebook, but there are probably dozens of notifications running in the background that you don't even know about, nor do you even need to. Getting rid of them is easy; go to Settings, then to Notifications. Anything that shows up as In Notification Center is currently active on your tablet. To disable them, tap on the app and then switch it to off. They aren't gone for good; anytime you want to turn them back on, just go to the very bottom where it says, Not In Notification Center and switch them back on.

Brightness

Turning down the brightness just a shade can do wonders for your tablet and might even give your eyes some needed relief. It's easy to do; go to Settings, then to Brightness. Just move the slider to a setting that you feel comfortable with.

Email

I prefer to know when I get email as soon as it comes. By doing this, my tablet is constantly refreshing email to see if anything has come in; this drains the battery, but not too terribly. If you are the kind of person who doesn't really care when they get email, then it might be good to just switch it from automatic to manual. That way it only checks email when you tap the Mail button. To switch manual on, go to Settings, then to Mail, Contacts, Calendars and finally go to Fetch New Data. Now go to the bottom and tap Manually (you can always switch it back later).

Location, Location, Lo...Battery Hog

Have you heard of location-based apps? These apps use your location to determine where you are exactly. It's actually a great feature if you are using a map of some sort. So, let's say you are looking for somewhere to eat and you have an app that recommends restaurants, it uses your GPS to determine your location, so it can tell what's nearby. That is great for some apps, but it is not so for others. Anytime you use GPS, it's going to drain your battery, so it's a good idea to see what apps are using it and question if you really want them to. Additionally, you can turn it off completely and switch it on only when needed. To do either, go to Settings, then to Location Services, switch any app you don't want to use this service to off (you can always switch it back on later).

Accessorize

90% of you will probably be completely content with these fixes and happy with their battery life; but if you still want more, consider buying a battery pack. Battery packs do make your tablet a bit bulkier (they slide on and attach to the back of your tablet), but they also give you several more hours of life. They cost around $70. Additionally, you can get an external battery charger to slip in your purse or briefcase. These packs let you charge any USB-C device. External battery chargers cost about the same, the one advantage of a charger versus a pack is it will charge any device that has a USB-C, not just the iPad.

The easiest way to save battery life, however, is to go to Settings > Battery and switch on Low Power Mode. This is not the ideal setting for normal tablet use, but if you only have 20% of your battery and need it to last longer, then it's there.

Chapter 10: Accessibility

When it comes to accessibility on the iPad, there's a lot you can do. To simplify things, I'll break it up into four short sections:

- Vision
- Interaction
- Hearing
- Media & Learning

This will make it easier to skip whatever isn't relevant to you.

Before I get to any of that, where exactly do you find Accessibility? What's great about Apple products is you find things almost the same on any Apple device—which means the way we find Accessibility here is the same way you find it on Apple Watch and iPhone.

So where is it?!

First, tap the Settings icon.

Next, go to Accessibility.

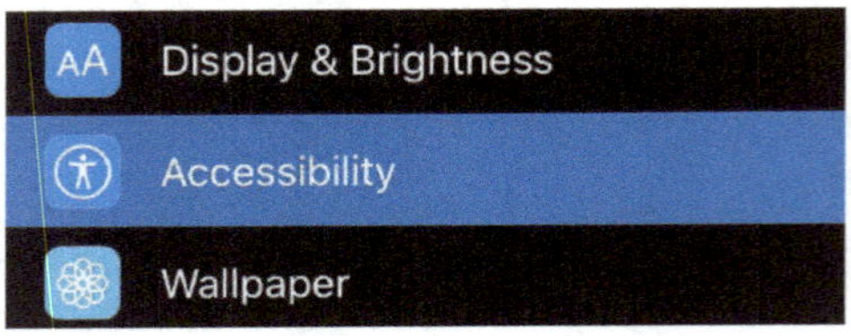

Vision

Vision accessibility features take up more than any other feature. If you're sitting there thinking, "I can see just fine," I'd still recommend checking this out. There's more here than just seeing—you may see perfectly fine, but still prefer text a little larger or bolder.

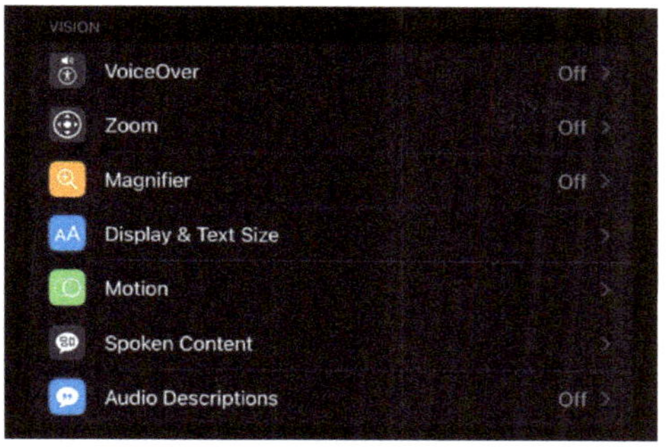

I'm going to go through the list of accessibility features you should know about below and, if necessary, how to use it. Some will be pretty self-explanatory.

First up: VoiceOver. To access it, just tap VoiceOver.

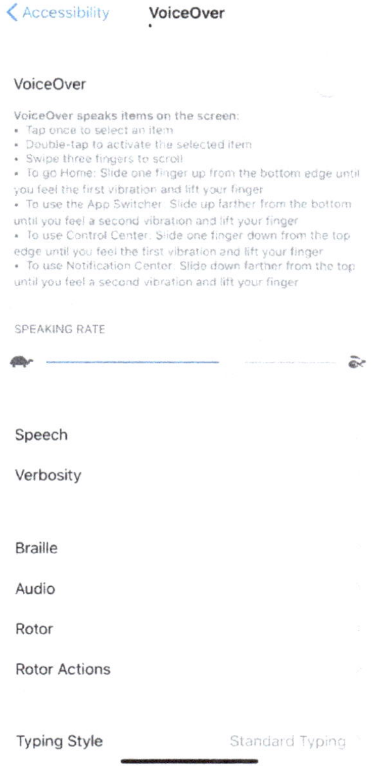

VoiceOver reads everything that happens on your screen. What do I mean everything? Exactly that! If you adjust the volume up, then VoiceOver will say back to you that the volume has turned up.

Turning this on is simple: flick the toggle. Controlling this feature? Not quite as simple. Turning it on means several of the normal gestures on the iPad are changed a little.

To go Home, for example, you swipe up until you feel a vibration; if you want to switch apps, you swipe up a little further until you feel a second vibration.

The person reading things back is probably a little too fast by default. To slow him down a bit, use the slider under Speaker Rate. The closer to the turtle icon you get, the slower it will be.

If you like VoiceOver, but don't like how long it takes for him to read something back, you can make him a little less wordy by tapping on Verbosity.

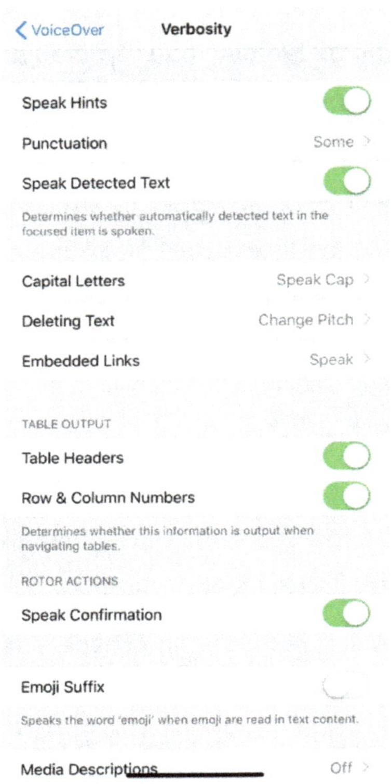

Braille is an interesting feature on the iPhone. You can't exactly feel braille on your phone after all. So how does it work? To use it, you need a braille reader that connects to your phone (usually via Bluetooth).

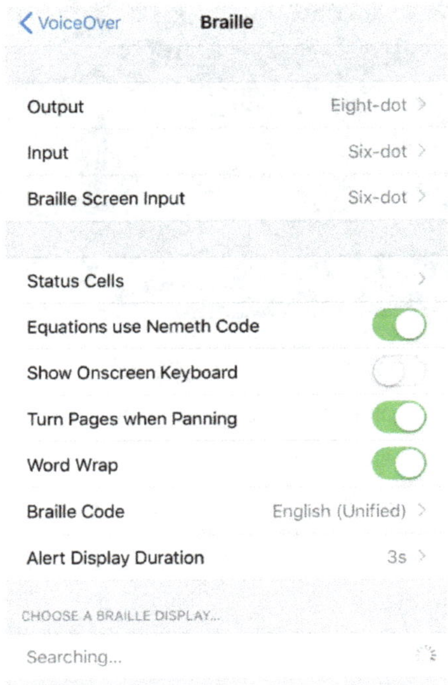

What else about VoiceOver do you need to know? The features under Braille will be a little less commonly used. Rotor controls actions you'll take to receive VoiceOver; Always Speak Notifications toggled on will read back any message you get automatically.

If you decide to use this feature, there's a number of third-party apps that are built for it. Just a few: TapTapSee, Seeing AI, Voice Dream Writer, Read2Go.

Below VoiceOver is Zoom. Zoom is a bit less intrusive than VoiceOver; it turns on only when you tap the assigned gesture, so you might forget that it's even on.

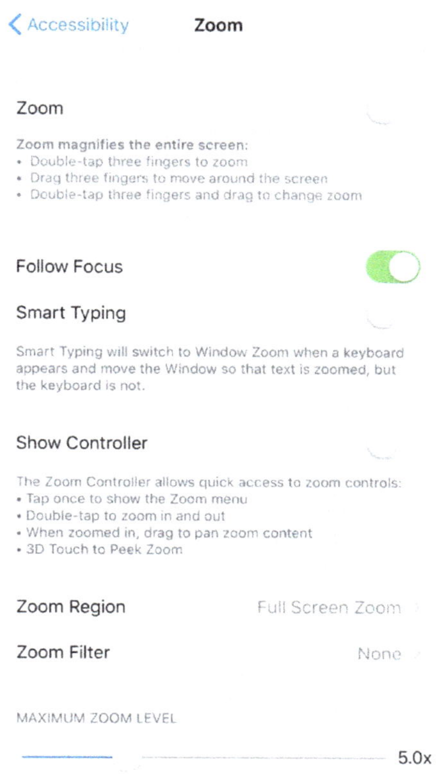

Once you toggle Zoom on, you can activate it at any time by double tapping with three fingers. Take note there: three fingers! Use one finger and this isn't going to happen—three fingers have to touch the screen. To exit Zoom, repeat this.

At the bottom of the screen, there's a slider to adjust the zoom level; by default, it's 5x; you can go up to 15x.

By default, when you tap with three fingers you'll get a small zoomed in window; want to see the entire screen? Go to Zoom Region and select Full Screen Zoom.

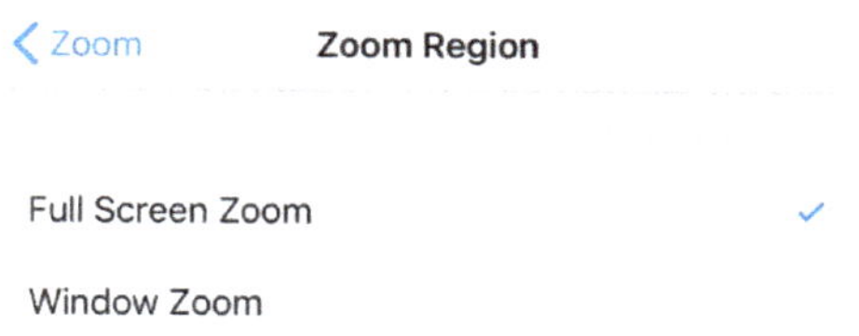

If your phone is in color, but when you zoom, you want it in greyscale—or any other filter—you can change that in Zoom Filter.

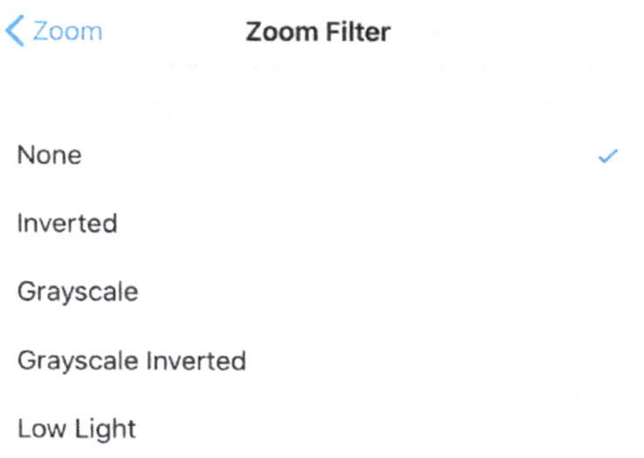

Below Zoom is a handy little feature called Magnifier.

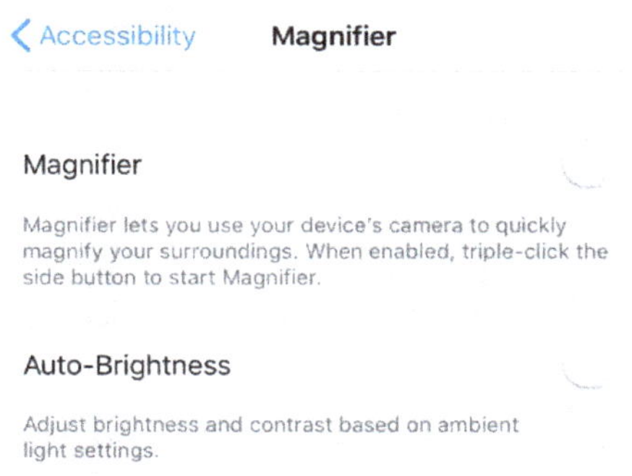

When you switch the toggle to on, a shortcut is added to use your phone as a magnifying glass. Triple-click the side button and a magnifying app opens up.

Near the bottom of the screen is a slider to adjust the zoom.

Display Accommodations is where you can make your screen black and white—or a number of different settings. Just go into Display Accommodations, select Color Filters, toggle Color Filters to on, and select your color scheme.

In Display Accommodations, you can also reduce the intensity of bright colors, turn off auto brightness, and invert colors.

One of the most common accessibility features is Larger Text; when turned on, this increases the font size for all compatible apps. On the bottom of this feature is a slider—adjust it to the right to make the font bigger, and to the left to make it smaller.

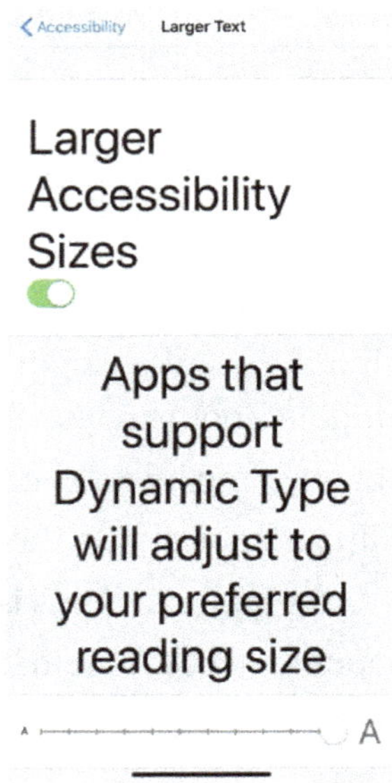

Finally, Reduce Motion makes the interface a little less—motion-y! What do I mean? The easiest way to explain this is for you to go to your Home screen. Move your phone around. See how the icons and background appear to be moving? If that annoys you or makes you dizzy, then toggle this on to turn it off.

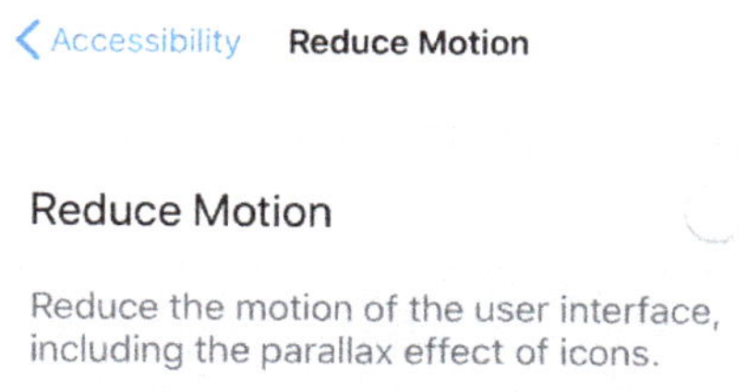

Physical & Motor

Interaction is the area that pertains to gestures and the things you touch on the phone to launch different apps and widgets. Some of these require special accessories that do not come with your phone; it will note this when you tap on the feature.

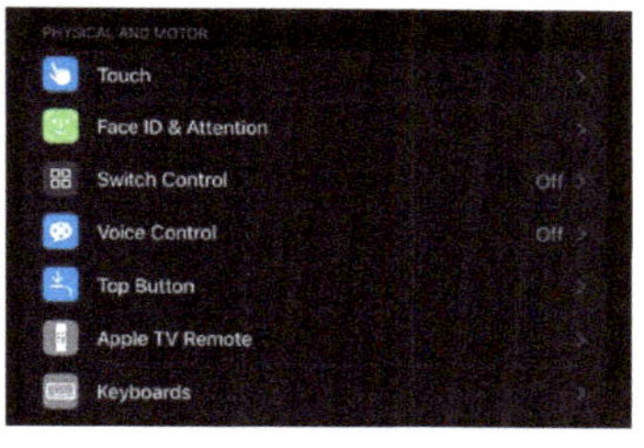

For the most part, these features will help you if you have difficulty touching the screen and find that you often open or type the wrong things as a result.

AssistiveTouch can use a special accessory, but it doesn't require one. When turned on, it turns on a round shape on your screen that works a bit like a large cursor. Tapping it opens up the box below and holding it will close the app. If you really miss that Home button on the phone, then you can think of it like a virtual home button—it even looks like one. Tap it once to bring up the menu and hold it to return to the Home screen.

Does Siri never understand you? You aren't alone. I once asked Siri to call my wife and she tried to call John. No idea who John is or why it sounds like "wife"! If you'd rather type to Siri to prevent that kind of mishap, you can turn it on here.

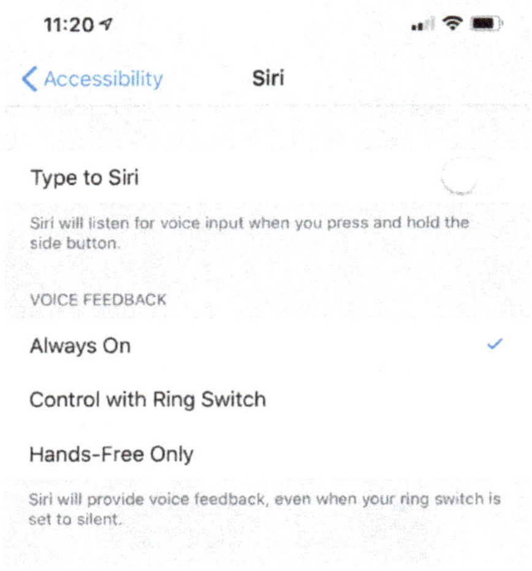

AssistiveTouch is also were you can change the settings if you'd like to use a Bluetooth mouse with your iPad.

Hearing

If you are using a hearing aid with your phone, then you'll add it and make adjustments to it in this setting. If you are looking for an alternative to a hearing aid, some people use Apple's own AirPods. If you want to do this, then it's recommended that you use third-party apps such as Petralex Hearing Aid. My suggestion, if you want to try this route, is to find cheaper earplugs.

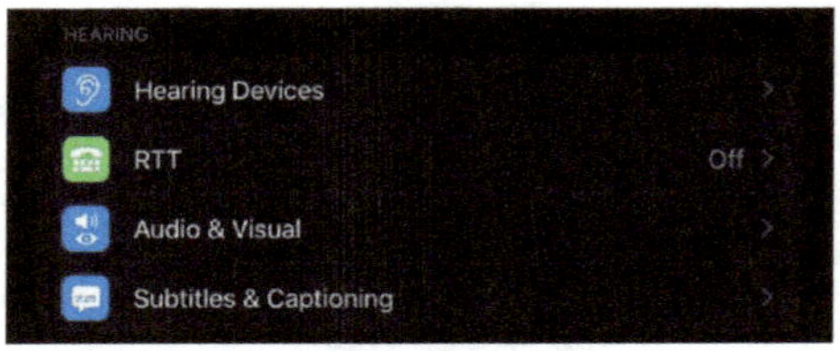

General

The area of this section I think is most useful is Guided Access. With this option turned on, you can triple-click the side button and turn on a blocked version of the app. What does that mean? It means you can turn off specific areas of an app, so if someone is using the app, they can't click certain buttons. Personally, I use this option for my child; she likes to FaceTime, but has a tendency to hit buttons like Hang Up; I turn on Guided Access, then restrict that button.

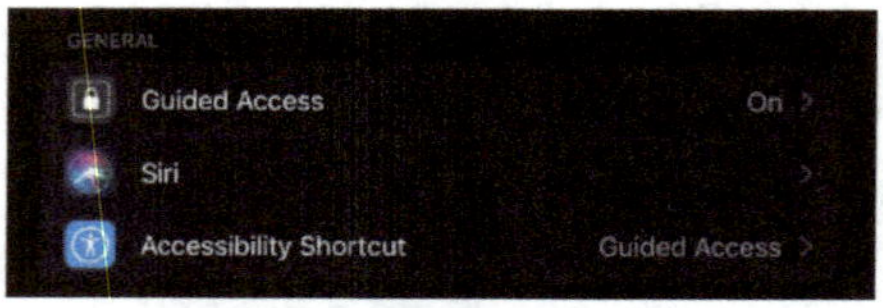

Appendix A: Accessories

Apple Pencil

The biggest companion to the iPad—perhaps the reason you bought the device—is the Apple Pencil. The Pencil looks like a normal stylus, but it's much more sophisticated than that; there's actually a tiny processor inside of it and when you use it, it's scanning for a signal over 240 times a second.

Unlike other styluses, the Apple Pencil has a battery built into it. To charge it, simply connect it to the magnetic side of the iPad. Apple says you can get 30 minutes of life into the Pencil by charging it for just 15 seconds. Don't worry about constantly charging it, however—it will last roughly 12 hours on a full charge.

Using the Apple Pencil is also easy; as soon as you touch the Pencil to your screen, the iPad can sense that it's a Pencil and not a finger. Pressing the Pencil harder on the iPad will make the line or object you are drawing darker; pressing it softer will make it lighter. If you want to add shading, tilt the Pencil; the sensors inside the Pencil calculate the orientation and angle of your hand.

Scribble for Apple Pencil

Apple Pencil got a huge upgrade in iPadOS 15 with a new "Scribble feature that lets you use the pencil in search fields —so you can scribble text in a Google search, for example, instead of typing it out.

You can use Scribble anytime there's a text

If you type something wrong, or want to erase it, just put a squiggle line through it.

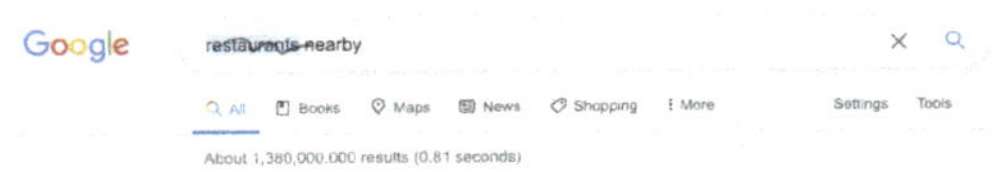

If you want to highlight a word or sentence, circle it.

You can also connect two words by putting a dash between the words.

Using Apple Pencil With the Notes App

When you use Apple Pencil with the Notes app, Scribble works differently. You are still technically scribbling text, but you are not going to see that instant conversion.

In Notes, Apple Pencil treats the app like a journal, and keeps your handwriting intact.

That's not to say you can turn your scribble into text—the process is just a little different. After you have wrote out the text, tap and highlight it with your finger just like you would any normal text. When the box comes up asking you what to do, select copy as text, and then go to where you want the text to go and paste it.

The Apple Pencil is pretty sophisticated, but if your handwriting is as bad as mine, then there's a bit of a learning curve.

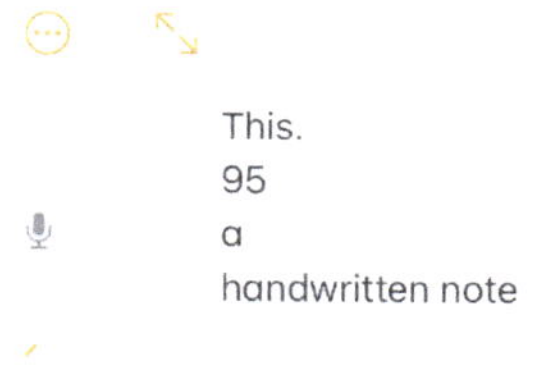

Apple Pencil isn't just for text. It also can also recognize and convert shapes. To use it, draw a shape (i.e. circle, square, etc) as you normally would, and when you get to the end, pause, but don't lift your pencil —just pause. In seconds, it will show a preview of how it thinks the shape should look; if you are satisfied then lift the pencil.

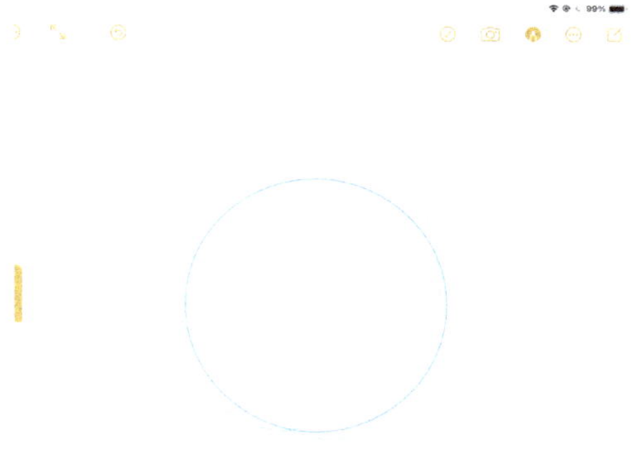

Apple Pencil Settings

Apple Pencil settings are limited. You can access them, but going into the Settings app, and selecting Apple Pencil.

From here there are two settings you should be aware of. The first is "Double Tap"; when you double tap on your Apple Pencil it does something—what it does is decided by you here.

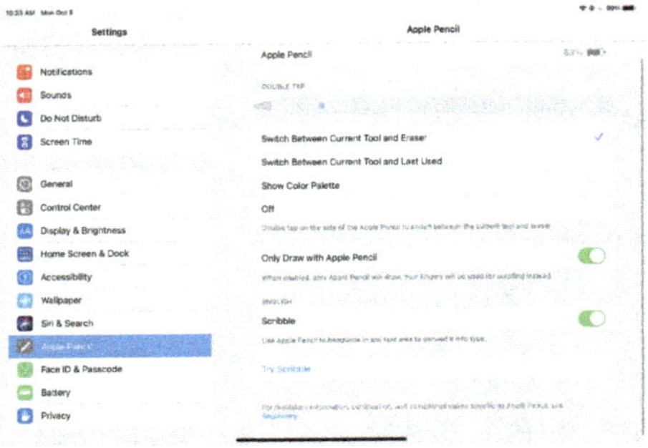

The second thing you should be aware of is Scribble; if you absolutely hate the feature or just need it off for a short period, then tap the toggle switch.

Smart Keyboard for iPad

The Keyboard is full-size—meaning it's the same size and spacing you are used to on larger tablets. Being full-size means there's room for shortcuts. Holding down on the CMD button next to the space bar, for example, while you are in Pages, brings up the menu below:

Bold	⌘ B
Italic	⌘ I
Underline	⌘ U
Copy Style	⌘ option C
Add Comment	⌘ shift K
Find	⌘ F
Hide Word Count	⌘ shift W
Hide Ruler	⌘ R
Create Document	⌘ N

If the Keyboard isn't sturdy enough for you, another keyboard to check out is the Logitech Create keyboard; it's about 10 dollars cheaper than the Apple Keyboard, but works the same way. The Logitech keyboard has a backlight (so you can see the keys in the dark) and charges through the iPad, so there's no need for batteries. It comes at a cost, however—it's about a pound in weight.

Bonus Book: AirPods

iPad is great for listening to music…sort of. To get the most out of the iPad, it helps to have wireless headphones or air buds. Yes, you could use the sound that comes directly out of the phone, but that's not ideal when you are exercising, in public, or in an otherwise loud place. This section will cover one of Apple's most popular solutions to this problem: AirPods.

What's Right For Me? AirPods or AirPods Pro

AirPods Pro is $50 more than the normal AirPods's. What exactly are you paying for?

Both, afterall have a H1 chip; both have wireless cases, and both have 24 hours of charge time with the case—the AirPods actually lasts longer than the Pro (5 hours of listening vs. 4.5).

What gives?!

There's a couple of advantages that the Pro has and that is what you are paying for. For starters, the Pro comes with three tips for a better fit. The AirPods's have a universal fit. My wife, for example, can't wear the normal AirPods's because her ears are too small; the Pro's fit perfectly.

The AirPods Pro is also sweat / water resistant—that's not to say you should go swimming with them (don't!), but it is to say if you are having a heavy work out and start to sweat, or it starts raining a little on your walk home, you don't have to take them out.

Noise cancellation and transparency modes are exclusive to the AirPods Pros.

The Pro also has Adaptive EQ; if you want to know what that means, look it up. It's a technical way of saying it sounds better—noticably better.

If you like charging the old fashion way (not wirelessly), the AirPods has what "some" might consider an advantage: it's normal USB where the Pro is USB-C. Everything is changing to USB-C, but if you are still living in an old USB world, then you won't have to buy any extra adaptors to make it work.

WHAT'S IN (AND NOT IN) THE BOX

AirPods come like every other Apple device—in a very minimalist box. The section covers the AirPods Pro. What's inside the AirPods box is similar with two important details: the charging is not USB-C, and the Pros have tips.

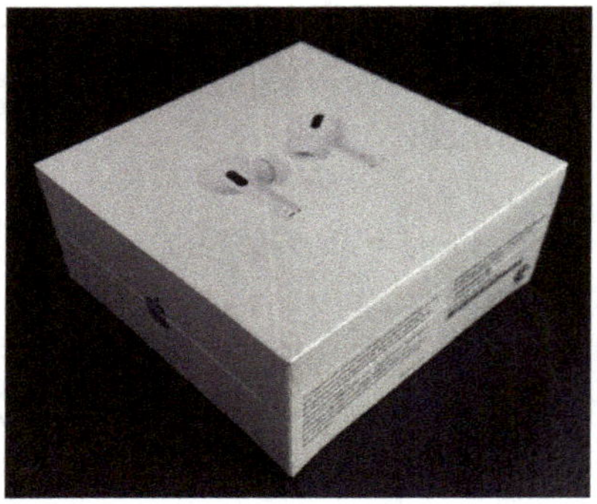

The first thing you see when you open the box is a very short guide that tells you how to use the device. It doesn't tell you everything—it's a high-level overview.

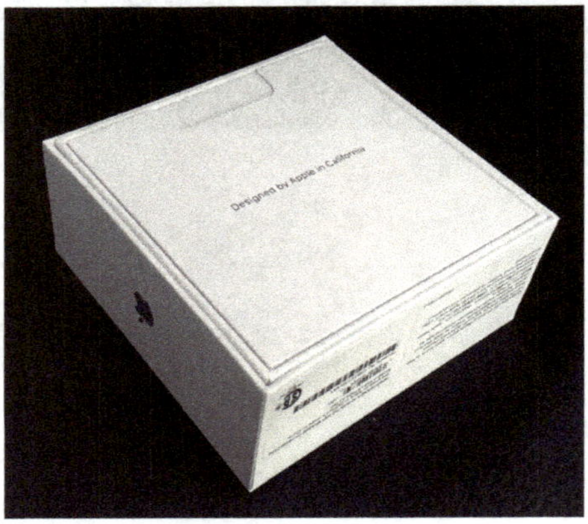

Below the instructions is the AirPods case (which also contains the pods).

Be careful as you lift out the case or you might miss the ear tips that are underneath it. The medium tip is already on the AirPods; if you want a smaller or larger tip, you'll find them here. Replacing them is as easy as pulling them off, then pushing the new ones on. The AirPods will automatically configure the sound based on the size you are using.

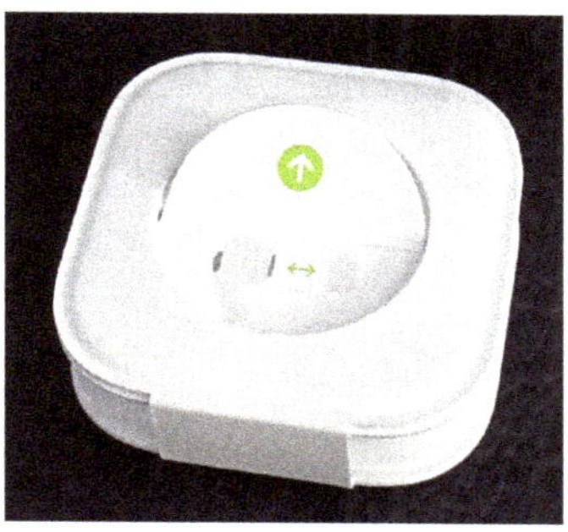

Finally, underneath the tips is the charging cable. Note the word "cable" here. There's nothing to plug it into. You'll have to supply your own. There's also something else very important here—it's lightning to USB-C. What does that mean? If you have a regular old-fashioned iPhone, then this won't plug into your charger. You need to get a USB-C adaptor to plug into. They aren't that much, fortunately, but it's still an inconvenience.

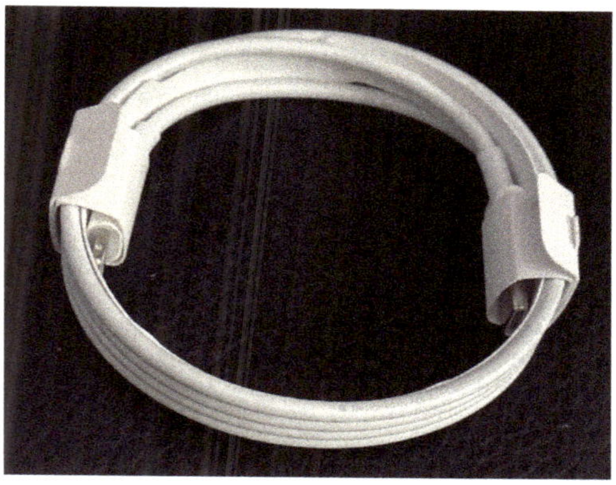

Setting Up AirPod Pro

Setting up your AirPods is a unique experience. It's ridiculously simple! Are you ready?

Unlock your iPhone. Put the case next to your iPhone. Open the case. That's it! This will launch a welcome screen on your iPhone automatically that will self-guide you to pairing them.

If you haven't updated your phone recently, then you'll get a message about limited functionality. If you want all the features to work, then update your phone to iOS 13.2.

You can see what version you have (and update it to the latest version) by going to Settings > General > Software Update. Software updates are usually quite large, so expect this to take at least an hour.

Assuming your phone is updated, you'll see some info about how your AirPods work. There is no skip here. You can either read it or ignore your phone a few seconds until it is gone.

Near the end of the setup, you'll see a message about Announce Messages. You can turn this on or leave it off (you can turn it on later). Basically, this gives Siri permission to read messages to you without you having to unlock your phone. It's helpful if you are working out and don't want to take out your phone to read a message.

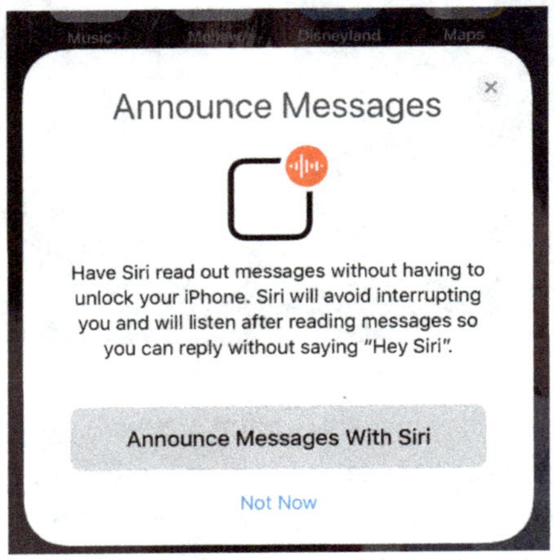

Once you connect your AirPods, you will see how much power is left in them; you can see this any time by opening the AirPods case next to your phone.

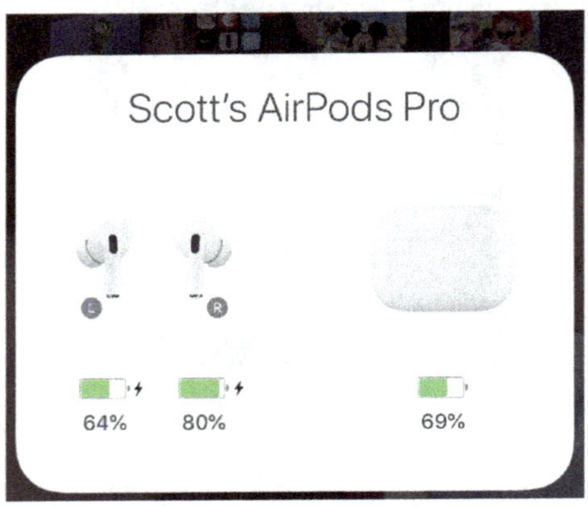

Once you add your AirPods to your phone, it adds them to iCloud. That means you can now connect them to any other Apple device (iPad, Mac, Apple Watch, etc.).

On any Apple device, go to how you would normally connect to Bluetooth (see the below illustration for connecting on a Mac), and select connect. If you are listening to something on your iPhone and tap this, it will unpair the iPhone and pair the new device.

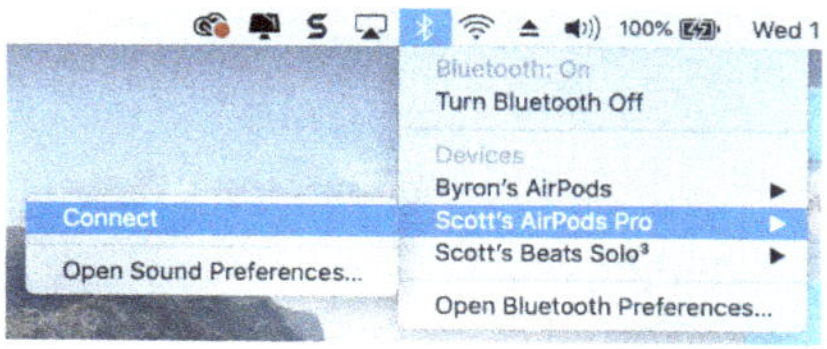

Setting Up AirPods

Setting up standard AirPods starts the exact same way. Make sure your Bluetooth is on, put the AirPods next to the iPhone, and open the case.

The biggest difference in the experience is after you tap connect, you're basically done. There's no message if you haven't updated your device, there's no tutorial, there's nothing about Siri. There's a message about how charged your device is and a done button. That's it. Tap done and you are connected. Anytime you put them in your ear from here on out, it will automatically connect.

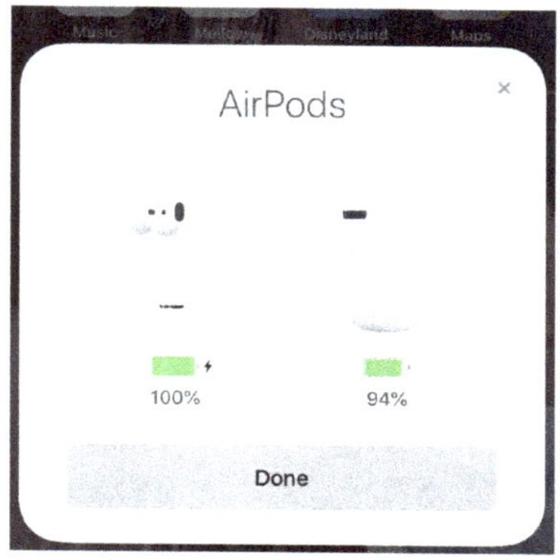

Manually Pairing

You can use AirPods on non-Apple devices (such as Android phones or games); you can also manually pair them to other Apple devices that aren't your own.

It's actually a similar process to pairing any other Bluetooth device.

The first step is to open up the AirPods case; when it's open, press the round button on the back of the case and don't let go. When the LED light inside the case begins to flash, you are in pairing mode.

Now go into your Bluetooth settings (on an iPhone it's Settings > Bluetooth). It will show the device. Tap on it, and it will pair. To unpair it, just tap on it again, and tap Forget This Device.

Factory Reset

To factory reset your AirPods, make sure both of the AirPods are in the case, then open the lid. Next, press and hold the round button on the back of the case for at least 15 seconds. You can stop when you see it flashing an amber color.

AirPods Pro Gestures

Controlling your AirPods Pro is all about gestures. To activate any of these gestures, push the long stem of the AirPods Pro. These are the main ones that you should know:

Play / Pause – Press once. This also works to answer incoming calls.

Skip track – Press twice.

Go back track – Press three times.

Active Noise Cancellation / Transparency mode – To toggle between these modes, press and hold until you hear a noise.

Hey Siri – Siri is activated the same way it is on any other Apple device—by saying "Hey Siri."

AirPods Gestures

AirPods are a lot more simplistic then AirPods Pro. Where the Pros have several gestures, AirPods have one: double tap.

Double tap by default activates Siri by default. In the Changing Settings section, I'll cover how to change this to Play/Pause, Next Track, Previous Track—or turn it off entirely.

Control Center

When connected to your AirPods, you can also control your device from the Control Center (swipe down from the upper right corner). Press and hold on the sound control for your AirPods; this brings up an option to toggle Noise Cancellation / Transparency mode.

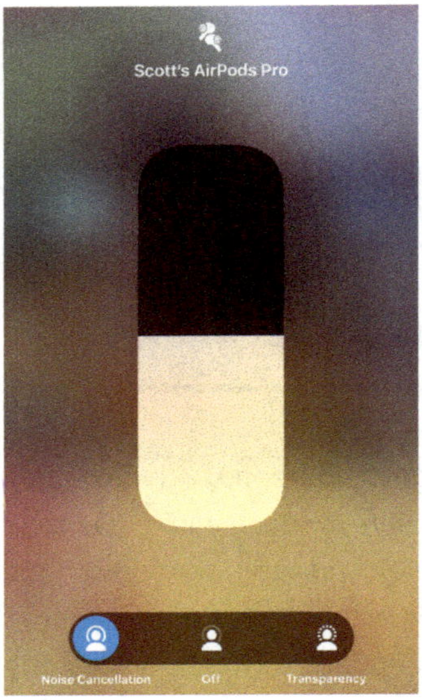

When music is playing, you can click on it from control panel and bring up an option to share audio. This lets you connect multiple Bluetooth devices to your device—so you could have two AirPods connected.

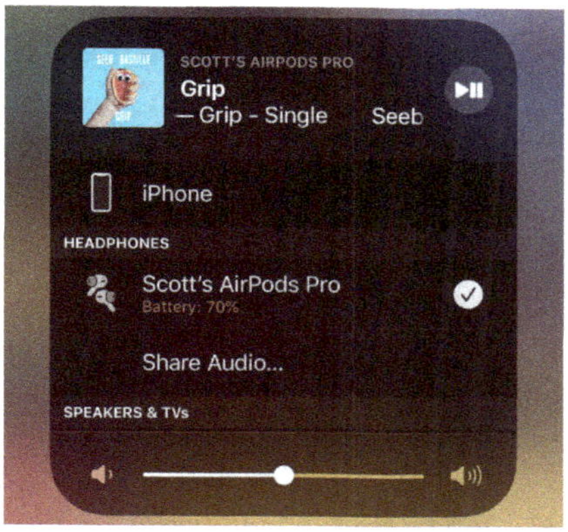

Changing AirPods Pro Settings

There are a number of things you can configure on the AirPods Pros, but you need to have them connected to your phone. If your AirPods is setup with your phone, but not currently connected to your phone, then you will not see the next steps on your device.

To get started, go to Settings > Bluetooth. Under My Devices, tap on the (i) next to Connected.

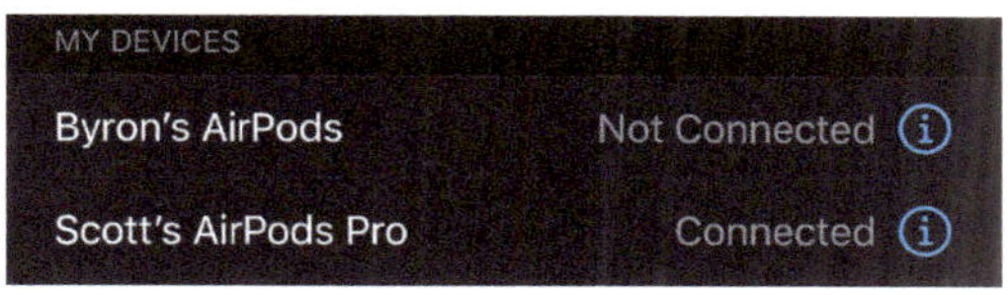

This brings up several options. If you want to unpair the device, for example, select Forget This Device. If you want to rename it, tap on the name in grey, then rename it.

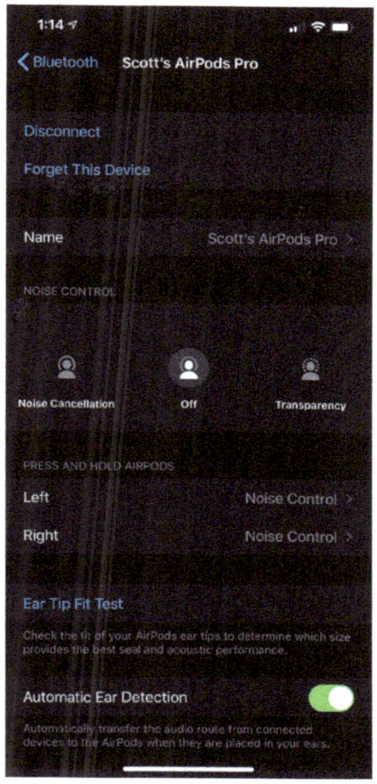

What I suggest starting with—before even using your device—is Ear Tip Fit Test. The AirPods are pretty smart, and they can make sure you pick the tips that fit you best. When I first used them, for example, they felt fine; I didn't even bother trying another tip until I ran the test.

To get started, tap the blue Ear Tip Fit Test.

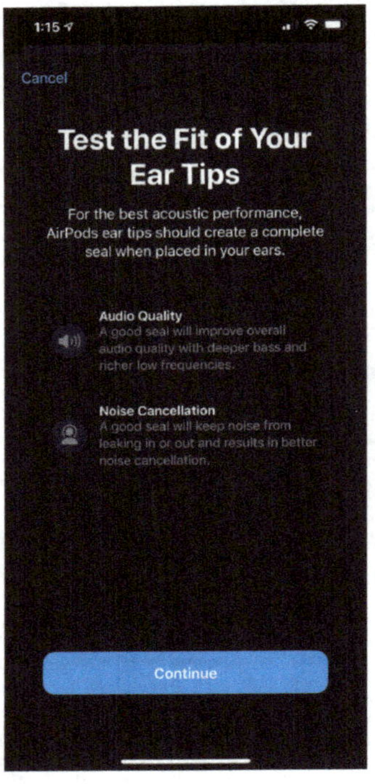

Once you hit continue, it will tell you to put each AirPods in your ear, and then press the play button.

You'll hear a song playing. After a couple of seconds, you'll see a screen with the results. My results say something went wrong. I either have the wrong tip size, I didn't push the AirPods in enough, or they're in the wrong ear.

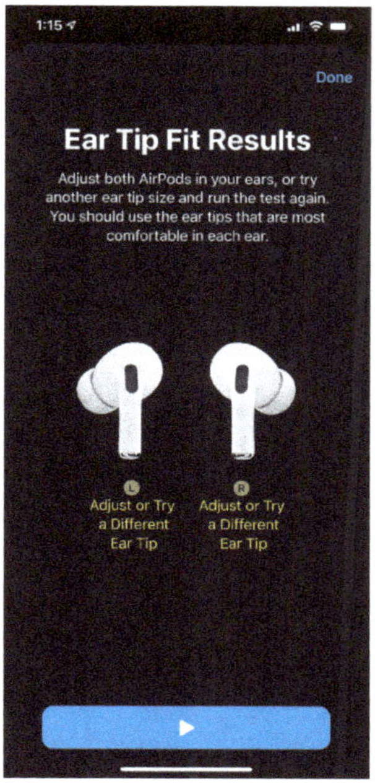

In my case, I knew they were put in right and they were in the right ear. So I put on a larger tip. Once you do that, push the play button again to run the test. With the bigger tips (medium in my case) the results said it was a good seal.

Changing AirPods Settings

There aren't as many things you can change on the AirPods, but there are a few.

To get started, go to Settings > Bluetooth. Under My Devices, tap on the (i) next to Connected.

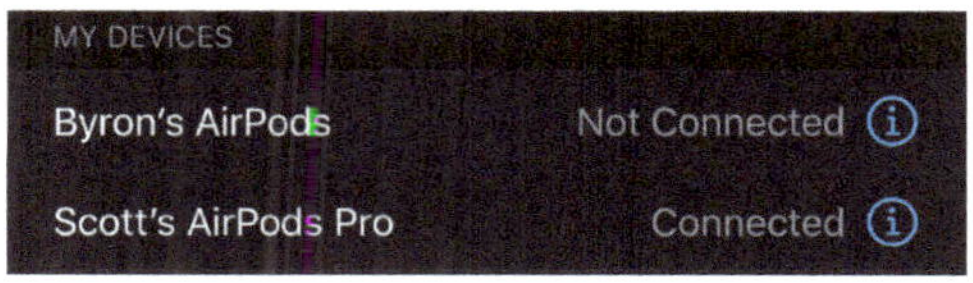

This brings up several options. If you want to unpair the device, for example, select Forget This Device. If you want to rename it, tap on the name in grey, then rename it.

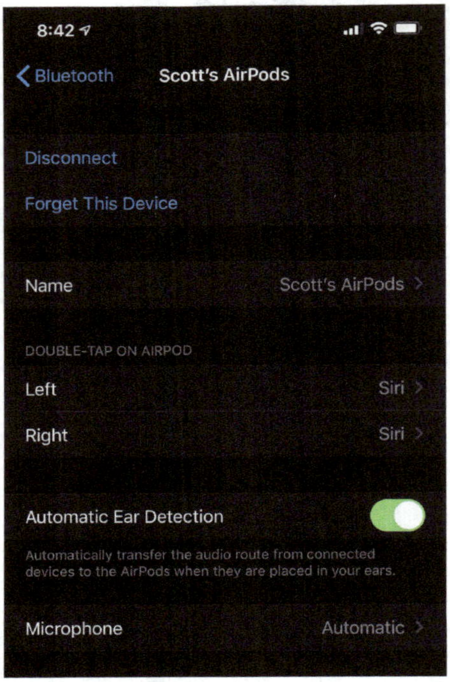

The setting you should pay most attention to is the Double-Tap on AirPod. This lets you change the tap gesture from Siri to something else—you can do one per AirPod, so technically, you get two gestures.

Once you make your selection, just tap the back button. It saves automatically.

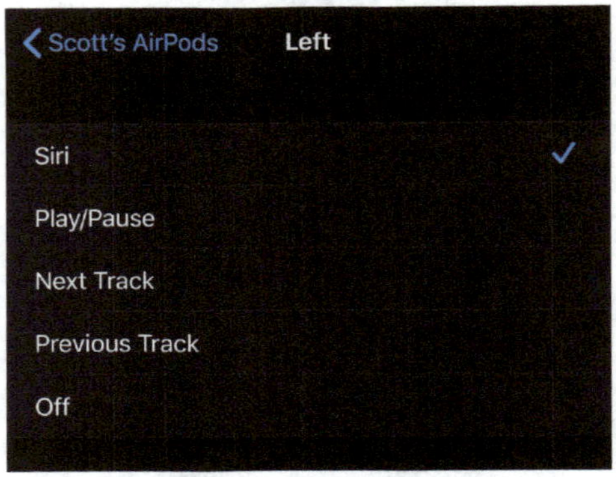

One other setting you may want to change is the microphone; by default, the AirPod will automatically detect the best AirPod to use when you are talking to someone on the phone. If you prefer to select this, then this is where you would do so.

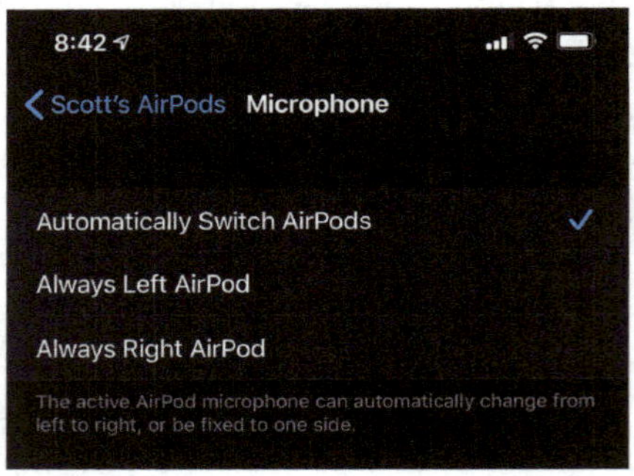

Accessibility

Unlike normal AirPods settings, you can control accessibility settings without connecting to your AirPods.

To get started, go to Settings > Accessibility.

Next, tap AirPods.

From here, you can adjust the Press speed, the Press and hold duration, and use Noise Cancellation even if only one AirPods is in.

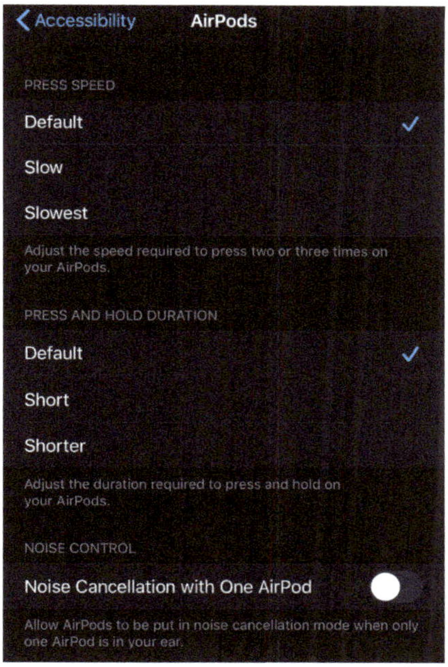

Hearing Aid Apps

AirPods are great for music, but they can also double as a hearing aid.

While the intent of the AirPods is certainly not to replace a traditional hearing aid, that hasn't stopped a number of developers from creating apps that help you use them as such.

Hearing aid apps actually work with any Bluetooth connected headset. That could be the expensive AirPods Pro, or the cheap headset you got at a garage sale. As long as you can connect it to your iPhone, then it should work.

The apps will basically help you amplify certain sounds to make hearing easier.

One popular example is TruLink Hearing Control. There are dozens of others. I would recommend trying several and seeing which one that you like the best.

INDEX

M

N

O

P

S

T

U

V

W

About the Author

Scott La Counte is a librarian and writer. His first book, Quiet, Please: Dispatches from a Public Librarian (Da Capo 2008) was the editor's choice for the Chicago Tribune and a Discovery title for the Los Angeles Times; in 2011, he published the YA book The N00b Warriors, which became a #1 Amazon bestseller; his most recent book is #OrganicJesus: Finding Your Way to an Unprocessed, GMO-Free Christianity (Kregel 2016).

He has written dozens of best-selling how-to guides on tech products.

He teaches writing for the Gotham Writers Workshops in New York and UX Design for UC Berkeley.

You can connect with him at ScottDouglas.org.

CPSIA information can be obtained
at www.ICGtesting.com
Printed in the USA
LVHW050523011222
734192LV00007B/179

9 781629 175652